The Sovereign Child

THE
SOVEREIGN
CHILD

How *a* Forgotten Philosophy
Can Liberate Kids *and* Their Parents

Aaron Stupple
with Logan Chipkin

Conjecture Institute

THE SOVEREIGN CHILD

How a Forgotten Philosophy Can Liberate Kids and Their Parents

FIRST EDITION

ISBN 978-1-5445-4797-8 *Paperback*
      978-1-5445-4798-5 *Ebook*

For my parents. Thank you.

CONTENTS

PREFACE

THIS BOOK IS INSPIRED BY A PHILOSOPHY OF PARENTING called Taking Children Seriously, a noncoercive parenting movement that was co-founded by Sarah Fitz-Claridge and David Deutsch and was prominent in the United Kingdom in the 1990s. At the time, Fitz-Claridge was pursuing the radical idea that it was possible to raise a child with zero coercion. She familiarized herself with various schools of thought on children and parenting but found that none of them fully measured up. Eventually, she happened upon an unlikely collaborator who lived in her city, Oxford physicist David Deutsch. Deutsch is a world-renowned thinker for, among other things, establishing the theoretical groundwork for quantum computing. In addition to physics, Deutsch was attracted to philosophy, and in particular the philosophy of Karl Popper. In subsequent years, Deutsch added to Popper's work in epistemology, personal identity, morality, and aesthetics, all of which are detailed in his two books, *The Fabric of Reality* and *The Beginning of Infinity*.

Deutsch's views on personhood aligned with Fitz-Claridge's intuitions about childhood freedom, and the two of them started a movement promoting a radically noncoercive approach to parenting. Fitz-Claridge went to conferences and met with parenting and schooling groups, and she organized a print journal called *Taking Children Seriously* that had thousands of paid subscribers at its peak. The movement lost steam in the 2000s, but the content of the journals remained online as a half-functioning web forum when I stumbled upon it in 2018, just in time for the birth of my first child. Six years later, my wife and I have been applying this philosophy with all of our five kids. We consider ourselves enormously lucky to have encountered these ideas, and the purpose of this book is to share them with others.

WHAT IS TAKING CHILDREN SERIOUSLY?

The simplest way to describe Taking Children Seriously is to describe what it is not. Taking Children Seriously avoids the two questions that frame almost every other school of thought on parenting:

1. What are the necessary limitations, restrictions, or boundaries for kids? Where should the parent draw the line on what is allowed and disallowed?
2. How do parents enforce these lines, limits, and expectations? Should they use harsh words, positive reinforcement, time-outs, confiscations, bribes, or breathing techniques?

Taking Children Seriously steps away from all of this. It has no interest in what the best rules should be, or how to enforce them, because it has no interest in rules. When most people hear this, their first reaction is to assume Taking Children Seriously is a fancy version of complete permissiveness, a well-known and ancient parenting style otherwise known as neglect. Rest assured: Taking Children Seriously is not neglect.

So what is it? Instead of focusing on rules, Taking Children Seriously focuses on fostering understanding. Parenting is the process of supporting a child until they understand the world well enough that they can support themselves. What is the best way to foster understanding? To provide freedom and security for a person's creativity to discover how the world works. Rules limit freedom, and hence understanding, and therefore impair the parenting project.

This book is inspired by the themes in *The Sovereign Individual* by James Dale Davidson and William Rees-Mogg. Unlike the self-sovereignty that Davidson and Rees-Mogg outline, which requires huge, society-wide innovation, the self-sovereignty we might unlock for children can take root in any home, anywhere, by anyone of any financial status. The sovereign child doesn't have to wait for anything except a curious parent.

Chapter 1 begins with freedom around food, then Chapters 2 and 3 move on to sleep and screens. Chapter 4 takes an extended look at the problems with enforcing rules in general. Chapter 5 presents problem-solving as the formal alternative to rules. Chapter 6 addresses the counterarguments. Chapter 7 presents various additional applications of the philosophy to daily life. Chapter 8 takes siblings seriously. Chapter 9 offers ideas for shifting from rules-based parenting to problem-solving-based parenting. Chapter 10 presents the philosophy of knowledge—the epistemology—that underlies the entire book. Readers who prefer to start with the foundations are encouraged to begin here. Chapter 11 closes the book with an expansive view of parenting in the ancient past and distant future.

DISCLAIMER

Above all things, my parents wanted to raise happy kids, and they wanted our childhood to be better than theirs. They both came from close families, but they were bothered by some features of their upbringing and vowed to make improvements for us. They succeeded spectacularly, and I grew up proud of my family and our norms around freedom, autonomy, and standards for character. I couldn't be more grateful. And yet here I am writing a book that criticizes staples of our upbringing like rules, chores, and discipline. I worry that my parents will conclude that I regard my childhood similarly to how they regard theirs. Absolutely not.

There is no final, best way to parent. But there is improvement, and that is what matters most. My parents were very intentional about making progress, and they often talked with my brother and me about the challenges of doing better for us than their parents did for them. Within their lineage, they probably tried the hardest to improve their kids' lives, not just materially, but psychologically. I love my grandparents, but I doubt they gave it much thought, and I doubt their ancestors did, either. My parents took a gigantic step forward.

This book is the opposite of an indictment of them or any other parent trying to make things better for their kids. Rather, it is inspired by them. It is an attempt to take another step forward. This book aims to honor that commitment and love, not to belittle or shame parents. Any indication of shaming that readers pick up is unintentional.

Effective criticism requires clarity and concision, and for that reason the arguments in this book are presented directly, without preamble acknowledging that they are just guesses, might be wrong, and are not meant to be hurtful. Instead, readers are asked to keep this disclaimer in the back of their minds and append it to any argument in this book that reads like a personal attack.

To my friends and family: If anyone sees themselves in my criticisms or examples, that is unintentional. The anecdotes about my kids are real. All of the references to parents, grandparents, and extended family and friends are hypothetical and not based on actual people. I couldn't be happier with or more grateful for my kids' relationships with their extended family.

Lastly, I am a practicing medical doctor, but nothing in this book should be considered medical or psychiatric advice.

Chapter One

∝

EATING WHAT THEY WANT

EATING MAY BE THE MOST PERSONAL HUMAN EXPERIENCE. Its closest rival, breathing, lacks the richness and variety of all the many foods and ways to eat, enjoy, and *experience* them. Eating is a primal exercise of sovereignty—to control your own eating entails governing both your body and what goes into it—but also a vulnerability, since things that go inside you pose an incredible risk. It is constrained by and intertwined with the laws of chemistry and biology but is also profoundly subjective and nuanced. Tastes and eating preferences don't just mechanically develop the way a child's body does—they are cultivated and refined, they are bound up with almost every other aspect of life.

For children, eating is like walking and talking—kids will figure it out on their own without any "help" from the outside. To be sure, parents are obligated to *provide* food for kids, since they're incapable of acquiring it on their own. But the duty to provide food does not imply the right, let alone the injunction, to *control* food. Consider: We provide food for houseguests, but we don't try to control them with it. In fact, we do the opposite—we ask them what their preferences are and try to satisfy those, while also offering some new options that might intrigue them. And, as always, our guests are free to decline.

Controlling children's access to food is the norm today. "A good parent does not let their kid eat whatever they want." There are various rationales, but the general argument is that eating is only about nutrition and desire, and since kids don't understand anything about nutrition and the dangers of their own desires, parents need to manage it for them.

Parents don't just control their children's food, they control them *with* food. Since sweets are generally restricted, they become a default reward for any desired behavior, and their restriction a punishment for any undesired behavior.

Taking children seriously means not mediating their relationship with food. A parent simply cannot know how a child should eat, because they cannot know their hunger patterns and cravings or how different foods taste and feel to them.

Should parents really just let their kids eat whatever they want? The short answer is *yes*. Kids should have a wide range of foods to explore and learn about with no restrictions, limited only by what their parents are capable of providing. Outside well-known poisons or even borderline substances like alcohol, anything that adults eat should be on offer for kids. The reason kids should have free rein with regard to food is that they are building an understanding of how to eat in the same way that they are building an understanding of everything else in life: by exploration, discovery, and trial and error.

As adults, we have *reasons* for how and why we eat. Breakfast can be carefully orchestrated to support a workout, or scarfed down in the car so we don't get hungry at work. We can show off our favorite brunch spot, or casually order in from home.

Eating accentuates an endless variety of contexts—holidays, potlucks, birthday parties, cookouts, school lunch, movie theater snacks, Halloween candy, religious observances. To reduce food to simplistic binaries—healthy or unhealthy, natural or unnatural, good or bad—is to misunderstand how the boundless *experiences* with food color one's life.

Given the central role food plays in daily life, rules around eating can be particularly damaging. It is common, perhaps even the norm, for otherwise well-adjusted adults, having been raised with food rules, to have guilt, shame, and insecurity about eating. It is hard to imagine something more damaging to a life well lived than anxiety around eating.

The best argument I've heard for controlling food comes from the fear of kids becoming overweight. Eating may be deeply embedded in biology, but modern food is different. It is carefully designed to be inexpensive and taste good, with lots of sugar and additives that provide quick bursts of calories in place of slower-burning, heartier foods that were present in the ancestral environment that our bodies evolved in and for. So, without a parent's watchful eye, kids will eat junk food all day and get fat all too easily.

This concern is understandable. But it's not a good reason to enforce rules around food.

First, like every other understandable concern, identifying the problem is not the same as identifying the solution. Food rules often backfire: Rules might produce the exact eating compulsions and disorders that they are intended to prevent. As with rules around drugs and other dangerous substances, no strategy around food can guarantee that a kid won't become overweight. On the contrary, some strategies—in particular, those that entail rule enforcement—are *guaranteed* to cause suffering, confusion, and/or psychological damage.

Second, since weight gain is an unavoidable risk of modern life, the safest approach is for the child to develop a robust understanding of all aspects of food (cultural, biological, and personal) by engaging *directly* with the problem situation. An experience that is mediated by someone else prevents such discovery. Consider: Not being overweight because your parents forbid you from overeating is worlds apart from understanding your own desires and cravings and tailoring them to suit your other preferences for how to live your life, including body size and appearance.

A crucial guard against risk is to have a trusted and knowledgeable person available for questions. This lifeline can only work if this person has the child's best interests at heart, *and only if the child believes this*. Ideally, all judgment, expectations, and moralizing are absent. If a kid finds themself struggling with food issues, a parent should be there to help by offering knowledge, guidance, and any other kind of support they might need. Fear of punishment, shame, or even more rules only push the kid to find potentially dangerous work-arounds, like eating disorders, or to cope with their issues via psychological torment, like hiding food.

Third, a robust understanding is not only critical to safety but also to living well. With respect to food, this means eating in a way that supports other interests and preferences, including one's *own* conception of health, relationships, ambitions, and avocations. I know foodies who will travel internationally just to eat exotic dishes, and I know people who consume mostly meal replacement drinks in a bottle so they can minimize the time spent preparing and consuming food. Each of these suits their particular lifestyles, which they've developed over years of exploring the world—and that exploration begins in childhood. None of them would be well served by someone forcefully intervening and telling them the "right" way to eat, whether now or back when they were children.

The would-be intervener might—*might*—be able to guess what a child's tastes and preferences are in the moment, but they definitely can't know how those tastes and preferences will evolve. If a parent forces their own preferences into the process, this will clash in some way with the child's developing desires, cravings, needs, and interests.

There is nothing wrong with exposing a child to your preferences. Quite the opposite. The key is allowing them to reject your preferences. If they aren't allowed to opt out, then your preference necessarily disrupts their understanding of the world. If vegetables are unwanted, then being forced to eat them would cause resentment toward the person doing the forcing. Vegetables wouldn't only be about their taste and texture and how they make the kid feel, but they'd also be about the person who forced it and guesses about that person's expectations and anxieties. Forcing always introduces confusion, extra layers of problems to solve, or both. Hardly a recipe for learning about food or anything else.

What would *I* do about my kid's weight? First of all, I'd wait until it appears as a problem before addressing it. Eating a second ice cream cone won't immediately make a kid overweight. Neither will a third or even a fourth. In fact, it might make the kid sick to their stomach and teach them about satiety far better than a parent's speech could. Put differently, overeating might provide its own signal for why not to overeat. By waiting for obesity to present itself, related discoveries about overeating are made available that would otherwise be blocked off by food rules.

The truth is that there is a lot of time to wait and see if a pattern of eating is causing a problem. My five-year-old son has been eating ice cream almost exclusively for the past few months, and, if anything, he's on the thin side. Before ice cream, his staple was Oreo cookies, but he seems to have grown tired of them. He eats ice cream as a meal, and he goes many hours between servings, not because we limit him, but presumably because he only likes to eat a limited amount at a time. Over the course of a day, he consumes a typical amount of calories. Contrary to popular opinion, free rein simply does not guarantee excessive eating of sweets or any other kind of food.

By giving him free rein, he has learned how to feed himself—he gets the ice cream out of the freezer that sits below our fridge and spoons out his own serving. Everything about the food that he eats is mediated by *him*, uncomplicated by judgment, expectations, or rules.

If my kid did start to become overweight, I'm not sure I would do anything about it out of fear that he would think I disapprove of how he eats. Tension with meals and snacks adds up over time, and there's no guarantee that it would be worthwhile. I've seen parents nag their overweight kids to no discernible effect except misery and humiliation. Instead of doing something, I'd wait until my kid *himself* expressed dissatisfaction with his weight. Once my kid identified that he had a problem, by his lights, and made it clear that my support was welcome, only *then* would I help him problem-solve by exploring the problem situation and guessing possible solutions. Every step of the way, I would take extra care to make it clear that I'm only here to help him manage his weight and eating issues the way he wants.

What about bad eating habits? What about addictions to foods designed to hook us to their sugary and fatty ingredients that evolution did not equip us to handle?

There are several reasons why this is not a good argument for restricting food. First, as I said before, there is the usual risk of backfire: Forbidden foods become extra tempting.

Second, rules confuse kids about how foods work. For instance, eating unlimited lollipops can teach you that doing so is kinda gross. It makes your tongue raw, your mouth sore, and your stomach upset. My kids have access to practically infinite lollipops, and they rarely finish even one. They are ages three to six, and they basically see lollipops the way I do: tasty at first, but not worth it after ten or twenty licks. But if I limited their lollipop consumption, they could never discover any of this.

Building on this, the third reason is that avoiding or overcoming bad habits requires *understanding*, not mandatory avoidance. For example, to avoid overeating cookies, you have to understand that cookies can be delightful with tea after dinner but don't satisfy hunger enough to substitute for a real meal. To discover this about cookies, you need to try them out.

Moreover, because I am not a gatekeeper or adversary with my kids, they are open to my suggestions about food. They don't think I'm trying to manipulate them when I tell them that *I* don't find cookies to be filling. My kids often take my insights seriously and change their eating choices accordingly. For instance, they tend to trust my suggestions that they eat more in preparation for a long car ride or finish a serving of yogurt that would otherwise spoil. Since these requests are tethered to the reality of food and not some arbitrary set of rules, and since they always have the option to refuse, they *build* up my kids' understanding rather than block it.

Lastly, it is inevitable that kids will encounter cheap processed food. Is it really better to shelter them from it, allowing just a few indulgences, merely to delay the inevitable? Is a sudden exposure to the full range of junk food in their late teens a good way to teach restraint?

WHAT ABOUT MAKING SURE
YOUR KIDS ARE HEALTHY?

Is it possible to let a kid eat whatever they want and have them grow up perfectly healthy, with frictionless relationships with food and with themselves, all the while making no sacrifices in terms of your relationship with your kid? Yes, if you can be the helpful problem solver rather than the adversarial gatekeeper, if you can patch over rough spots by, say, supplementing nutritional deficiencies with multivitamin gummies or figuring out a few "healthy" dishes that are made genuinely appealing. I'd rather try that than badger my kid about what they eat at every meal and snack opportunity, knowing full well that badgering might not even work.

HUNGER

A common objection is that parents must manage their kids' hunger, otherwise life will be difficult for everyone. If kids just eat junk food, then they never get satiated and are always hungry and irritable. This perspective often hails the virtues of eating "real food," which is vaguely defined as any food that is heartier, more traditional, more filling, and more nutritious than the admittedly tastier artificial foods on offer.

A major problem with this approach is that controlling a kid's food can *cause* irritability. It can produce anxiety and moodiness, even for kids who "eat well." A key observation that drove me away from enforcing food rules was witnessing all of the strife generated by making kids "eat right." It struck me as a losing strategy to battle with a toddler until they've eaten sufficient amounts of approved foods in a bid to avoid battles with irritable kids later on. Why not let them eat what they like and see if battles arise at all? If not, it's a glorious win–win. Why not have sufficient amounts of junk food always on hand so that kids can eat whenever they're hungry? If you're concerned with nutrition, why not search extra hard for natural foods that they like, or processed foods that are somewhat hearty? One solution we've found is chocolate bars and Nutella, both of which are appealing, travel well, are easy for kids to manage themselves, and have enough fat to be relatively filling, especially when combined with other foods. We decided early on that we wouldn't fight with our kids about food in order to forestall fights with our kids about hunger. Instead, we'd deal with hunger and the corresponding possible irritability when it arises.

I suspect that hunger is used as a rationalization for why kids are irritable and moody, when really they are chafing at rule enforcement in general. Any time a kid gets defensive, it's easy to blame a lack of "real food" or a lack of sleep or too much screen time. Food rules become a useful tool for control in terms of other rules. In general, parental force causes its own problems whose proposed solution is even more force.

FOOD CULTURE IN A HOUSE WITH NO RULES

My basic approach to food with my kids is to treat them like I would houseguests who didn't choose to visit. I prepare for them the food that my wife and I eat but also ask if there are different foods that they prefer. If so, I'm sure to stock the house with those foods. After all, when vegetarians visit, we make vegetarian food. On the other hand, I wouldn't consider myself a slave to whatever they demand. I make an effort to prepare meals that they like, including wasting a bit of food and remaking meals that are rejected, but only to a point. Eventually, I'd throw in the towel and tell a picky eater that they're on their own—though I make sure to keep a store of foods that they tend to prefer.

All of the kid food in our house is stored at knee height in open cabinets and in the easy-to-open freezer so the kids can always see what's available. This includes cookies and ice cream as well as more wholesome foods like noodles and fruit. There is no secret location for candy and no embargo on juice.

If my kids want to skip a meal, I don't lecture them about eating now so they don't get hungry later. Instead, if we are taking a trip, we bring plenty of snacks in case they get hungry. I'll often put breakfast in front of my kids and ask them to eat it in preparation for a trip, but if they refuse, I take care not to give the impression that I'm displeased.

We don't make our kids come to the table for family dinner. That's not to say we don't care about shared meals—we certainly value this bonding experience. In fact, we value it so much that we don't want our kids to develop resentment about it. We want them to participate in shared meals for the same reasons *we* want to do it, and those take time for a small child to discover. We encourage them to join us, we try to make things like setting the table and preparing the food fun and special, and we let them bring their tablets or toys to the table. My two daughters almost always join in, but my son rarely does. He doesn't like a fuss and prefers to eat at his own kid table at a time of his choosing. I am confident that he enjoys our company and will eventually join in the family meal, and I'd much rather wait until he comes to this conclusion on his own.

One of the best consequences of giving kids free rein with food is that it eliminates a source of conflict among siblings. Our kids don't guard their treats from each other, nor do they taunt or tease each other when one of them has a treat that the other doesn't. If they want more, they can always have more.

There is never a complaint that something isn't fair because no one has limitations. Instead, my kids take joy in each other's delights and preferences. Any time I'm in the store with just my oldest, she loves to pick out the snacks that her brother and sister like. Another happy consequence is that I can eat whatever I want in front of them. I always feel bad eating sweets in front of kids who are restricted, so it's a relief not to have to hide my consumption in order to appear that I'm following the rules.

All that said, I think there's something else going on here. Even if parents weren't concerned about health, or diet, or getting enough energy, many would still seek to control food. There is a sense among parents that kids should have limits set on things they want, *because they want it* and *regardless of what that thing is*. I call this sense that it is wrong for a child to satisfy their wants the Greedy Child Fallacy. This idea is not usually spelled out so explicitly by parents, but it has evolved over centuries and manifests so frequently that we take it for granted.

Controlling the knobs on a kid's access to the thing they want can be used to control the child without resorting to more stigmatized methods such as physical and verbal abuse. Food is something that basically everyone wants, and so parents feel justified by the Greedy Child Fallacy to control their kids' relationship with food. But it's no more wrong for a kid to want to control his own food choices than it is for any other person.

The idea that children are inherently and destructively greedy is used to justify all manner of control. The parent isn't just right to deny access to things the child wants, but they have a *duty* to keep the child within some limitation or boundary, regardless of where that boundary is. After all, so the argument goes, children need to learn that you can't always get what you want. This "lesson" is often delivered with "tough love," despite the fact that it is irrational and not at all loving. An unsatisfied desire is a problem, and all problems have solutions. We adults spend our days seeking solutions to all of our problems, and we very often succeed. Imagine consigning ourselves to this or that shortcoming, because "we can't always get what we want." Outsiders will typically chalk such a defeatist mindset up to lack of confidence, unfounded pessimism, or failure of imagination—in other words, to false ideas that one can overcome.

Why can we not get this particular thing that we want? Why must this particular shortcoming be accepted? Is it bad to want the thing in question? If so, why? To be sure, desires can be either good or bad. The reason behind the desire plays a huge role in determining a desire's moral character, not the mere fact that you can't always get what you want. The truth is we should always try to get what we want. When our desires are damaging, it's crucial to understand *why* they are damaging so that we can change course and pursue new and better desires, not apologize for being desirous in the first place. If we block this process by needless fiat, we are stuck with a desire that grinds away in the background as we force ourselves to try to ignore its allure.

CONCLUSION

Fortunately, everything seems to be going well in our household. Our kids are all within normal weight. Our daughters have palates at least as broad as that of a typical kid, and they genuinely enjoy all of the foods they eat. Since their palates are authentic, they are progressively refining their tastes, rather than forming preferences based on their parents' expectations. I have not detected anything like a sugar high after they eat sweets, and I'm convinced this is one of many tropes that have evolved to exert control. They do seem to get grumpy when they're hungry, but so do kids who are restricted by conventional food rules. And again, since they manage their eating without our input, they can make the connection between mood and food themselves. When someone is angry and irritable, they don't want to hear about how they should eat better or sleep more, and when they are pressured to fix the problem by eating or sleeping, this can trigger defensiveness that obscures rather than reveals the connection. As with adults, so with kids.

Chapter Two

SLEEPING WHEN THEY WANT

THE ARGUMENT AGAINST CONTROLLING SLEEP IS THE same as that of food, albeit quite a bit simpler. Sleeping, like eating, is deeply and irreducibly personal. Just as it is impossible to know what another person's tastes and cravings are, it is impossible to know how tired a person is and how that compares with other preferences they have at any given moment. Like eating, sleeping needs to be figured out, and kids need to become attuned to the signals coming from their bodies so that they can make the appropriate trade-offs between staying awake and getting rest.

Imagine a good friend is visiting from out of town. You are tempted to stay up late to spend time with him, but you also have a project due tomorrow morning at work. Or imagine you have started a movie, and it is so gripping that you consider staying up later than you'd planned to finish it. Or maybe you're trying to add exercise to your daily routine, but the only time to fit it in is at dawn. The idea that there is a simple rule to follow across all of these problem situations is nonsense. In each case, the correct choice depends on a broad consideration of priorities, preferences, and the unique workings of one's individual body. It is common to both regret staying up late and feel selfish for going to bed early. The best we can hope for is to learn from our mistakes and refine our choices moving forward.

In fact, it is those very experiences that often teach us about the value of certain friends, the quality of particular movies, and the utility of exercise. Walking around bleary-eyed at work can feel almost satisfying when it is caused by spending time with a great friend. Or, if the late-night hangout session was a bore, if your friend was uncaring about overstaying their welcome, then the sense of fatigue the next day might spark frustration and cause you to reevaluate your friendship. If you're often staying up and finding yourself miserably tired at work, maybe that's because you hate your job. If you find yourself excitedly jumping out of bed to exercise, maybe your late-night activities are worth dropping.

Navigating these trade-offs through trial and error is how we figure out our preferences and arrange our priorities, a process otherwise known as living our lives. Simple rules like "get eight hours of sleep a night" tell us nothing about the relevant trade-offs and actually block our ability to rethink and fine-tune our preferences.

These considerations are even more important for children, who, unlike adults, are in the process of discovering the very idea that they are the owners and stewards of their preferences and priorities. Autonomy is much more than the pleasure and pain of making good decisions. It is being the architect of your own life. Staying up late watching movies is only a problem in terms of what the kid wants to do in the morning, and the kid needs to be able to figure all of the relevant trade-offs themself. Like eating, fatigue and sleep are some of the most elemental features of life, as they touch on almost every experience one has in the course of a day. As such, it is crucial that a child have a direct relationship with them, unmediated by others and hence free from the distortions and confusions of considering what other people think. A kid can only come to truly understand how rest and fatigue impact everything else in the context of the freedom to try them out.

SCHOOL, SCHEDULES, AND SLEEP

The most common objection to letting kids manage sleep on their own is concern about waking up for school or day care. The argument is that kids aren't capable of taking these morning obligations into consideration, and so the parents need to do so on their behalf so that the kids aren't so miserable and exhausted during the day that their mood and performance suffer.

The short answer is that sleep is an excellent reason not to force a kid to go to school or day care in the first place. Getting enough sleep has as much to do with waking up as it does with going to bed. Lots of energy is directed at the circumstances around going to bed, but the necessity of waking up early tends to be taken for granted. It should not be.

Consider how different the life of a child is when they can sleep in every day. When there is no anxiety around going to bed, kids can enjoy themselves in the evening and continue engaging with whatever has captivated their interest. Parents, too, don't feel pressure to get their kids ready for bed. The sequence of bathing, teeth brushing, and pajama dressing is no longer a forced march that inevitably pits the resolve of the parents against their kid's desire to stay up and have fun.

Waking up for school sets in motion a schedule for the entire day *and for the whole family*. Parents need to pick the kids up after school, or arrangements must be made for after-school activities. These need to transition into dinner, which needs to be on the table in time for homework, which in turn needs to get finished before bedtime preparations. The entire day is on the clock, which suffuses it with tension that degrades everyone's ability to enjoy the moment or engage in a curiosity. A kid has no ability to sink their teeth into anything that requires more than an hour or so of attention, and priorities can't be rearranged because they are shackled to the schedule.

The beauty of a weekend is not just the luxury of sleeping in—it is the freedom to stay up and watch an epic movie, play a video game until your fingers ache, or horse around with siblings until everyone is bone tired. And that freedom suffuses the whole weekend. This is what childhood is *for*: the freedom to explore the world, discover and pursue passions, and generally "waste time" playing and daydreaming. Why would we want to limit that to the weekend?

On the other hand, the school-induced schedule creates an environment of anxiety and stress. Parents become taskmasters, and all the activities of a child's life are seen as temporary steps in a sequence that, if not maintained, might collapse at any moment into chaos.

Everyday tasks cannot be pursued for their own sake but rather must be tailored to the all-encompassing schedule. Kids can't eat food for pleasure or novelty but instead to have energy for the next activity. They can't try on clothes and new hygiene choices solely to look and feel good but instead to appear presentable at whatever is next on the schedule. Screens aren't about their content but instead about distracting from the scheduled activity, making them a harmful temptation rather than a beneficial window into the world.

Humorously, school is about college, and college is about getting a job and sustaining a life. And only then, *in your twenties*, can food and bathing and clothes and entertainment be about those things in themselves. Shouldn't childhood be the time when kids are free to explore those things that are integral to life, to learn about and develop relationships with them for their own sake? The magic of childhood is that kids don't have dependents or even a responsibility to ensure their own survival, so it is precisely during this time that a person is most free to engage with the world directly.

WHAT ABOUT PUTTING TODDLERS ON A SCHEDULE?

Even before school and day care age, it is common for parents to put toddlers and babies on a schedule, which means structuring predictable times for naps, eating, and play. A reliable nap time or bedtime is certainly helpful for a caregiver who has other things they want to do. However, the above arguments against schedules apply to toddlers and babies as well.

First, scheduling can backfire, especially with toddlers. Ironically, trying to get them to sleep at certain times so that a parent can structure their day around them puts severe limits on what *parents* can do. Nap times become a kind of fulcrum for the day, with a lot of anxiety centered on whether the parent can "get the kid down." If successful, quiet must be maintained to sustain the nap for the allotted time. Even in the best circumstances, this adds rigidity to things like hosting guests or accommodating spontaneity, since everyone is required to literally tiptoe around nap time.

Worse, when putting a kid to sleep doesn't work, parents waste hours trying to succeed, using up the free time that the nap was supposed to generate for the parent in the first place. If the child's resistance to nap time devolves into full-blown conflict, then the child tends to become even more restless than before. We discovered early on with our first child that spending hours trying to get her to sleep at opportune times rarely worked out. It was much more efficient to simply go about our day and figure out how to accommodate her if and when she fell asleep. This relieved us of the burden of trying to manage her, eliminated any conflict about getting her to go to sleep, and allowed her to develop her own sense of when she was tired and needed a rest.

What about small children who want to stay up and keep everyone else awake?

When toddlers stay up late, they still want to be entertained, and this is a problem for parents and siblings who want to sleep. It is hard to address this from afar because kids vary greatly in their preferred means of entertainment. In general, parents are not obligated to entertain their kids at all times. Just because kids have free rein doesn't mean parents are their slaves. When I feel like going to sleep, I tell my kids that I'm tired and that I don't feel like playing with them anymore. Then, just like adults, my kids find ways to entertain themselves with technology like iPads until they're ready for bed according to their own preferences. When I make staying up less interesting, my kids are less interested in staying up, too—after all, they regard me as a trusted source of fun in their lives. Taking your kids seriously gives them reasons to take you seriously as well.

TAKING BABIES (AND THEIR
MIDNIGHT CRIES) SERIOUSLY

What about babies at night?

When people hear you have an infant, a universal refrain is, "Is she sleeping through the night?" People's tolerance for being awakened from sleep varies widely, and for those fortunate souls who don't particularly mind, I suspect this isn't much of an issue. But for many people, being awakened is so disturbing that it is one of the scariest aspects of becoming a parent.

Like all problems, this one is solvable, and trying out all manner of tricks, like using white noise, glowing toys, and particular bedding and clothes, are all worth exploring. Nonetheless, these efforts often fail, leaving parents dangling at the end of their rope. At this point, many parents consider simply letting the baby cry it out. This is backed up by "the research," most famously the Ferber method. As with so many dehumanizing abstractions, "cry it out" suggests that babies crying it out is a mechanical process, like a leaf blower running out of gas, rather than a person in distress. Unlike the spent leaf blower, when a baby is left to cry herself to sleep, she is left to deal with her problem on her own. A baby crying herself to sleep marks a solution for the *parent*, but not for the *baby*. Babies are helpless, and a soothing parent is not some counterproductive crutch. If a crying baby is indeed a person in distress, then research showing an absence of long-term effects is irrelevant. I take ibuprofen for my headaches even though there are no long-term harms of enduring full-force headache pain.

One objection to worrying about a baby's state of mind is that babies don't seem capable of understanding or remembering. They seem like little more than prehuman blobs that we are imagining have more interiority than they really do. This is understandable, but consider the alternative. When during brain development do interior consciousness and rudimentary understanding flip on? My guess is that it's earlier than we think, and probably even before birth. I wouldn't be shocked if some basics of personality became established in the newborn and infancy period. I'm not going to explore the philosophical and neuroscientific features of this argument here. Instead, I take a simple, practical risk assessment. I would rather waste effort accommodating a newborn as if she can think about what's going on than treat her like an unthinking lump when she is not. You could call this "Taking Babies Seriously." Until we have some better theories about consciousness and explanatory thinking, this is the most prudent approach. After all, a baby is only a baby for a few months. Is it really asking too much to be extra cautious?

If babies are capable of rudimentary understanding, then when a baby cries out at night, they're doing so because they have a *problem*, not because of some biomechanical reflex. Perhaps they are scared or even have primitive fears about abandonment. Who knows? And who knows if an infant left to cry it out might form some long-lasting ideas about how (un)reliable their parents are? I wouldn't want to take a chance. I would hate for my child to form dark thoughts about the world because I thought they were too young to think.

Babies only have a few, simple needs. They didn't choose to come into the world and burden their parents with these needs—their parents knowingly burdened themselves. It seems wrong to signal to a person just beginning life that their needs aren't important.

On a practical level, I immediately comfort a crying baby. If this was disrupting my sleep, I would try to take daytime or morning naps, see if I could start work later, or extend a parental leave. I would consider hiring a night nanny, as the problem might go away in a few weeks. We wanted to bring our babies into the bed with us, but this raises the risk of sudden infant death syndrome, and we couldn't get comfortable with that idea. To get around it, we first bought a bassinet that attaches to the side of our bed, so it was easy to drape an arm in to comfort a crying baby. When we had twins, we bought a king-sized bed and placed a foldable travel bed between us so the babies could safely share a bed with us.

CONCLUSION

Like eating, sleeping is connected with almost every other thing one does in life. Living well requires adjusting and fine-tuning priorities when things change. Some preferences will conflict and others will complement, and these may swap when things change. Eating and sleeping come to bear on nearly all other preferences, and so they are among the most crucial things to learn about early in life. This learning should be free of confusion, fear or shame, and arbitrary moralizing. One's preferences around eating and sleeping should be as seamless as those for breathing and walking, although the former are far richer and more dynamic. It is therefore essential that parents not muck up a child's discovery process.

Chapter Three

WATCHING WHAT THEY WANT (SCREENS)

MY KIDS LOVE YOUTUBE, ESPECIALLY MY SON. HE HAS gone through four YouTube-fueled obsessions in his five years: jungle creatures, octopi and squids, sea mammals, and Godzilla. He spends several hours a day scrolling videos on the topic du jour and then recounting his findings to anyone within earshot. With unfettered access to his iPad, he hoovers up facts about the natural world, broadens his vocabulary, and develops his understanding of storytelling and characters.

Behind the scenes, the YouTube algorithm notices his choices and supplies him with endless content that matches his growing interests. He shares what he learns with us, and he uses it in his imaginative play. Some of his favorite toys are discarded household items that he repurposes to play-act what he sees on YouTube. As he cycles through various channels on various topics in various formats, he experiments with their speaking styles and turns of phrase.

This portal to his interests isn't just entertaining and edifying for *him*; it is incredibly helpful to *us*. When my wife and I are trying to get work done around the house, he doesn't bug us to focus on him. When we visit friends who don't have age-matched kids he could play with, he entertains himself with his iPad. When I need to disrupt whatever he's doing to run an errand, he is happy to oblige as long as he can watch something in the car. And when he wants to stay up late, he is content to watch his tablet while the rest of the family sleeps. YouTube obviates countless opportunities for family discord.

We all know the stereotype of the kid who spends too many hours staring at a tablet—isolated and withdrawn, distracted, unable to put the device down, and irritable when separated from it. His language is stunted, his relationships lack emotional depth and richness, and he is ignorant about the real world.

My son's reality is the total opposite. He is quick to exchange his tablet for a friendly face. He welcomes adults and siblings into his world for hours of imaginative play. People are impressed with his vocabulary. He consoles his little sister when she's upset and plays pranks on adults. And he knows a ton of stuff. I'm not saying YouTube is making him a genius, but I'm convinced it's not harming him, and I'm confident it is enriching his life far more than if he was forced to play only with wooden blocks and puzzles.

The biggest difference between our household and other households is how our kids eat, sleep, and use screens. At first glance, screens don't seem as fundamental as food and sleep, but they are—perhaps even more so. That's because screens are bound up with *attention,* which might be the most basic element of our autonomy. When we lose everything, the last thing to go is control of our attention.

At the heart of adult resistance to screens seems to be the idea that adults have a right, even a duty, to control what children pay attention to. Attention is the simplest manifestation of what a person cares about, and intruding on their attention always signals that their values are less important than the intruder's values. Adults communicate this awareness to other adults with phrases like "Pardon the interruption," but with kids, it's often assumed that the interruption is rather a necessary redirection or correction.

Like so many truisms of conventional parenting, this one has things completely backward. The role of the parent is to support children's growing autonomy, to nurture it with engaging problem situations, and to be there to avoid injury when mistakes inevitably happen. It is not to step on their autonomy indiscriminately. Parents might object that their control of children's attention is not at all indiscriminate, that it is directed toward avoiding particular harms or some other superficially lofty end point. *But the child doesn't know this, and so it will feel indiscriminate and arbitrary to them.*

Nearly every misconception about children in general is revealed by how adults manage children's use of screens. All of the usual tropes are at work: kids can't be trusted, they don't know what's good for them, it's dangerous, it's bad for them, it's addictive, it corrupts them. Addressing all of these misconceptions thoroughly would be a book in itself. Instead, I will focus on the standard objections to unfettered screen use.

WHAT ABOUT CROWDING OUT REAL-LIFE EXPERIENCES?

Many of us worry that time spent on screens is time not spent reading books, exploring the outdoors, or developing relationships. What's worse, we worry that screens don't just delay the mastery of these skills, they may spoil them altogether if kids end up preferring virtual experiences to those in real life. If Facebook friends are always available, why get to know Grandma? Why learn to read if YouTube can just show you the content? Screens are so compelling that they might make the rest of life feel like a grudging necessity, something to be dealt with until the next opportunity to grab a screen.

The king fallacy at work here is the idea that kids gravitate toward drivel, that they prefer nonsensical garbage over substantive content. The fallacy suggests that multibillion-dollar tech and media companies are competing to produce content that is somehow perfectly stimulating—even addicting—but also empty. In this way, YouTube videos and the like are little different from fast food or cigarettes—designed to hook the consumer, regardless of the consequences. If parents don't intervene, kids will waste their days taking in this psychological equivalent of McDonald's or smoking.

The truth is that when kids are pursuing their interests, they are *always* learning, even if adults can't see it. Unfortunately, when it comes to adults assessing the merits of what their kids are doing, seeing is believing. When a child is constructing a jigsaw puzzle, an adult can see the physical manifestation of the child's mind at work. The child's mental effort is on display as she tries to connect a piece, fails, rotates it, and tries again. The adult can hear her groan when a piece isn't fitting and sense her joy when she figures it out. But when that same child is watching a cartoon, that same adult may take the kid's vacant look and physical activity as surefire signs that they're watching a fertile mind turning to mush.

But parents thought the same about books when novels reached mass audiences in the 1700s and 1800s. Biographies of Abraham Lincoln describe his father's anger at young Lincoln's obsession with books, which his father perceived as causing laziness and sloth.

Even the most rudimentary cartoon requires lots of mental effort for a young mind. The child needs to decipher the plot, how the different characters and elements in the scene relate to each other, how tone and gesture convey subtleties of meaning, what the characters' motivations are, and why the emotional consequences and payoffs make sense in the context of the story.

Solving a jigsaw puzzle is essentially one single, inert problem. In contrast, an episode of *Peppa Pig* is a thousand dynamic problems.

My guess is that adults fail to recognize this cognitive effort because they've seen the basic storylines depicted in children's shows countless times. The emotional lives of cartoon characters are often so thin that they seem superficial and annoying to adults, but kids are seeing these for the first time. For them, the depth may be just right. How do we know? Because kids are glued to the screen! A kid's interest is the prime indicator that the content is generating thought and learning.

Some children's programming is of particularly high quality, so much so that it also appeals to adults. It takes real genius to pull this off, which is why such content is rare. The bulk of what's available to children appeals only to children. As such, it should be judged according to whether it captures *kids'* interest, not in comparison to productions that adults find suitable.

Another fallacy is that children's programming displaces more sophisticated content. Again, it's the opposite. Children's programming is a *stepping stone* to more sophisticated content. When kids control their screens, they can watch enough immature content until they get bored and move on to something with more richness and depth. If, on the other hand, they are restricted to only deeper content that is beyond them, or worse, to bland and "educational" material, then they not only miss out on building their way to an understanding and appreciation of great art, but they may also come to resent it. How many people have been turned off from the classics because they were forced to read them when they were young?

A third fallacy is the idea that supposedly virtual experiences are less valuable than real-life experiences. By that logic, books should be restricted as well! In fact, so should *all* storytelling—after all, hearing about something is a poor substitute for actually doing it.

It's true that real-life experiences *can* be richer and better than digital experiences, but they also come with costs, such as the time and expense necessary to get to the right location, the opportunity costs of being unable to do other things, and risks of physical harm. Thousands of virtual experiences can be had for the price of one real-life experience. Many potential real-life experiences are simply out of reach, but anyone can watch footage from the Mars Rover.

Media is a portal to cultural knowledge, but adult gatekeepers have always been prone to moral panics about media's influence on children. Moral panics in the 1900s began with radio, then dime novels, television, comic books, rock and roll, video games, the Walkman, rap music, and topped off with the internet. In the twenty-first century, it's social media, YouTube, online games, and smartphones. So far.

One reason that this prejudice against virtual experiences carries weight is because it's such a useful tool for control. Parents can control their child's physical world much more easily than they can the world in their head, and hence many parents try to gatekeep the access points to their kids' imagination. Tablets pose a novel and currently unrivaled challenge to this type of control. Print media's physical form makes it easy for parents to restrict. Radio and television operate in plain view of everyone in the home. Tablets, meanwhile, are all-in-one, mobile, and private. In a world in which control over kids' experiences is assumed to be good, of course tablets—a portal to an infinite number of virtual learning opportunities—are regarded as poison.

Finally, many parents worry that screens will crowd out the unique learning powers of childhood. A child's ability to learn things like languages, musical instruments, and mathematics seems to drop off precipitously with the onset of adolescence. Perhaps staring at a screen during this precious time will deprive kids of a chance to take full advantage of their super-charged learning abilities that they will never get back?

This is a reasonable concern, but it leaves something out. If kids are remarkable learners during this time, then maybe they are learning lots of other topics that may be hard to measure. Perhaps they are uniquely open to new interests and are building a broad base for potential hobbies, passions, and careers. Many people trace the defining passions of their lives back to these formative years. In that case, screens can *expand* a kid's range of potential interests. Additionally, perhaps during this time, kids are particularly vulnerable to internalizing the negative effects of rule enforcement.

WHAT ABOUT ADDICTION?

The discussion of screen addiction has suffered from a confusion between two senses of the term *addiction:* the medical and the casual. The medical definition is precise: Addiction requires a chemical dependence on a substance and a self-injurious compulsion to maintain this dependence. The casual usage of the term is more of a general description of how much we like something and how much we are *seemingly* powerless to resist. Pretending that Grandma's cheesecake is addictive is a figurative device for exaggeration, but it's not anything like being hooked on drugs.

Unfortunately, given the stigma of addiction, it is frequently used as a smear tactic. Climate activists say we're addicted to fossil fuels, urban planners say we're addicted to cars, and health counselors say we're addicted to fast food. Exaggeration is fine, except when it is used to justify limiting others' freedom because they supposedly can't help themselves.

Alcohol offers a classic example of a true addiction. Chemical dependence gets established as alcohol binds to receptors in the brain, making its neurons less excitable. This dampens anxiety and induces a state of pleasurable calm. (Some drunks are not at all calm, because sometimes the dampening hits the inhibitions first, causing these drunks to become rowdy.) When the brain is consistently exposed to alcohol over time, it gradually reduces the number of these receptors, which means more alcohol is required to get the same effect. The structure of the brain is now dependent on a continual presence of alcohol, which is why alcoholics need to drink frequently just to keep calm.

What happens if an alcoholic suddenly stops drinking? The brain excitement that alcohol was suppressing comes roaring back, accompanied by withdrawal symptoms like tremors, sweats, and anxiety. Severe cases progress to florid delirium, accompanied by extreme agitation, hallucinations, and even seizures. Alcoholics become highly attuned to the first hints of withdrawal and become focused on finding another drink to avoid hours of misery.

This chemical dependence is key—everyone who is exposed to high doses of alcohol for prolonged periods will suffer withdrawal symptoms when alcohol supply is cut off. It doesn't matter what frame of mind they're in or what their intentions are; suddenly cutting off alcohol will produce withdrawal.

This isn't the case for pretend addictions like fossil fuels. It's common to take a break from fossil fuels, say, by taking a weeklong camping trip, and not experience anything like withdrawal. Many people who make a concerted effort to quit fast food report feeling better almost immediately. They may crave a Big Mac, but longing for something familiar is part of everyday life and is a world away from the physiological torment of withdrawal from a true addiction.

Now we can see that so-called addiction to the internet, video games, social media, and smartphones falls into the category of pretend. There is no chemical dependence or anything like universal withdrawal. Many video gamers simply get bored and move on to other endeavors. Some alcoholics do this as well, but they have to carefully wean themselves off over time, whereas gamers can simply walk away.

Repeated use of something may look like addiction from the outside, but that tells us nothing about what's happening inside the person's mind. I repeatedly use electricity, but I'm not hooked on it. I depend on it economically, not chemically.

People may spend a lot of time on various digital platforms, so much so that their friends and family get worried, but time spent on something doesn't unto itself indicate a problem. We all know people who spend inordinate amounts of time putting plants in the ground and fussing about keeping them alive, but we don't hector them about how addictive gardening is. A pastime, even an obsessional one, is a wonderful thing, and it's nobody else's business. Labeling those pastimes that violate *your* sensibilities as addictions misses the fact that everyone's interests and problem situations are infinitely unique.

We've seen how conventional parenting dismisses kids' interests as frivolous, unserious, addictive. Parents employ an entire arsenal of strategies to delegitimize kids' interests so that, whenever these interests collide with those of adults, the kids lose out.

This is not to say a disordered relationship with video games or social media is impossible—it absolutely is. But horror stories about kids retreating from life and engaging only with screens almost never address other things going on in their lives. The assumption is that the screen lured them away from an otherwise happy childhood and duped them into wasting their lives. When we hear of these reports, we almost never hear about other contributing factors, such as stresses in the home, issues with friends, or any of the myriad of things that can make kids seek out a refuge. In these cases, the nature of the refuge is not to blame. In fact, taking that refuge away without addressing the underlying problem simply makes things worse.

Finally, a common argument for addiction is that, when kids get irritable and restless when their screens are taken away, this is evidence that they are going through withdrawal. But I get irritated when the power goes out, not because I'm addicted, but because I need electricity in order to pursue my interests. What's more, if another person switches off my power just to thwart me, I might erupt into a full-blown rage.

Irritability and restlessness are reasonable expressions of resentment. Turning the tables on a child and citing their justified resentment as evidence of addiction is perverse. It commits the common error of only looking at the behavior and ignoring the reasons that *cause* the behavior.

This is the ultimate rationale for controlling children. It denies that they are people with interests, motivations, and values and falsely assumes that they are mere slaves to the chemical processes in their brains.

WHAT ABOUT DOPAMINE DEPENDENCE?

For many, dopamine has replaced drugs and alcohol as the bad-boy chemical. While in the 1980s and 1990s they used to bring in police officers to warn kids about the dangers of drugs, today they bring in psychologists and neuroscientists to warn us about the dangers of dopamine. Scaring kids about drugs didn't work, but chemical dependence on drugs is at least real. Dopamine dependence is not.

Dopamine is a chemical that operates in the reward circuitry in the brain. Every time you feel a sense of joy or euphoria, that feeling is accompanied by a rush of dopamine onto various regions of the brain. This fact has led researchers to implicate dopamine in supposed addictions to things we don't even ingest, such as behaviors like using the internet, video games, smartphones, and social media.

The claim is that dopamine serves as the chemical that our brains develop a dependence on, that dopamine functions in the brain of the social media user just like alcohol and nicotine do among drinkers and smokers.

Specifically, they claim that social media and smartphones are designed to trigger near-constant surges of dopamine that modify the nerves in our brains, making us go into withdrawal when these surges are taken away. They think that when addicts tap their phones and post on social media, they are desperately seeking a dopamine hit, and when they're deprived of their phones, their dopamine-starved brains go into withdrawal.

This is wrong for several reasons. For one, dopamine surges happen with *all* enjoyment, not just with superficial thrills.

Wholesome joys like playing with your kids or completing a project at work also involve dopamine. Can a person become addicted to being an involved parent or working hard at their career? When I'm away from my family for short periods of time, I feel compelled to return home. Am I a slave to the dopamine hit I receive when my kids greet me at the door? If so, this is a particularly dehumanizing view of human psychology, reducing everything meaningful in life to a chemical in the brain.

It's hard to make dopamine the bad boy when it is also embedded in everything that is good. Alcohol and nicotine can be extirpated from life, but dopamine cannot. Medicalizing dopamine as a trigger for disease makes people feel needlessly guilty and gives busybodies a license to stop people from having fun, ostensibly for their own good.

Second, since all joys require dopamine surges in the brain, the real question is: Which joys trigger dopamine in a way that is damaging? Answer: joys that come quickly and fleetingly, what is disparagingly called a cheap thrill. But we are famously bad at identifying these. Radio and comic books were thought to be addictive cheap thrills, and now we consider them wholesome. In fact, if fearmongers in the 1940s and 1950s had any inkling about modern neuroscience, they would have told us that dopamine was the reason that *Superman* comics were dangerous! Since we can't distinguish cheap, damaging pleasure from wholesome, healthy pleasure, we don't have a theory about dopamine addiction at all. Instead, we have a supposedly science-based cudgel that can be used to declare other people's pleasures as dangerous.

Third, truly addictive chemicals like alcohol, nicotine, and heroin exert their influence directly on the brain. Electronic devices and digital media, on the other hand, never even get inside our bodies, so the only way for them to influence the brain is through an intermediary. And that intermediary is *thought*. Before the phone can trigger a pleasurable dopamine surge in the brain, the user must figure out if whatever is happening on the phone is enjoyable. If, for example, your phone buzzes when someone likes your Facebook post, the amount of dopamine that surges in your brain will depend on what you think about the person who liked the post, how proud you are of that particular post, and the reasons you had for composing it. A like from a respected friend about something you care deeply about will produce more dopamine than a like from a mere acquaintance about something you posted in passing.

In contrast, addiction to alcohol and other drugs is unthinking. Alcoholics have been known to drink mouthwash and aftershave lotion, simply because once the alcohol is in the body, it will have its effect regardless of what the drinker thinks about it. Dopamine, on the other hand, is already in the body. The only way for something outside of the body, like a phone, to make dopamine surge is for the user to think certain things about what the phone is doing. If those thoughts change, if the user starts thinking this is boring, or that there's something else they'd rather do with their time, then the user can simply walk away.

If an alcoholic suddenly stops drinking, the withdrawal symptoms can be life-threatening. But heavy social media users have stories of just deciding to stop and moving on with no ill effects. Some report feeling better immediately, essentially the opposite of withdrawal.

What does all of this mean for children? I suspect that, deep down, few parents really think that their kids will become hopeless screen addicts. Instead, their primary concern is that kids will fall into a kind of pleasure trap, where they are captivated by a cheap thrill that proves unrewarding in the long term, and these kids grow up regretting the time lost. I know adults with such regrets. However, I also know adults who regret the time they spent in youth sports, learning the piano, and getting a useless college degree. It's not that sports, music, and college are traps (though social pressures can make them traps). The issue is that people waste their time on unproductive and unsatisfying pursuits when they don't have good reasons for what they're doing. Ironically, screens are a great way to get ideas about high-value pursuits in the first place!

What appears from the outside to be a pleasure trap might in fact be the beginning of a lifelong passion. On a societal level, comic books were once thought to be trashy, but now they're respected for their stories and worlds, their punch as humor or satire, and their artistry. And on the individual level, the determining factor is what the user thinks about comic books. One kid might enjoy a comic book for a few minutes and move on, while another might be intrigued and dive deeper and deeper. Furthermore, an interest in comics might ramify in several directions, such as developing an appreciation for drawing or art, or finding a taste for collecting or selling rare editions. Thinking, learning, and discovery can transform superficial pleasures into abiding passions and sustaining avocations.

A unifying theme is that no one can know ahead of time how a process of discovery will play out. This includes parents and other adults. Parents cannot know what's best for their children because they don't know what their children will discover about their own interests.

We see this phenomenon routinely depicted in stories and movies about childhood fascinations that are at first dismissed by adults, only later to be taken seriously when the adults see what the child has discovered. In these stories, there is often one very special adult character who acts as the child's mentor and guide, giving them support and confidence that there is indeed something worth looking for. My goal is to be that character as my kids explore the world.

ISN'T THE ALGORITHM DIFFERENT?

Tech companies have gotten very good at directing us toward interesting content. Are they too good? These companies track what we watch and click, analyze it, and then send us content that we're inclined to watch, click, and share. The software that pulls this off is menacingly referred to as "the algorithm," suggesting a computer overlord that manipulates users because it knows us better than we know ourselves. The worry is that these algorithms have hacked the human brain, are able to feed us content that is irresistible, and can control our choices about how to click, buy, and even vote.

First of all, modern tech platforms are not the first to identify principles of what makes content engaging. Dale Carnegie wrote *How to Win Friends and Influence People* in 1936, and it sold because the principles that he identified were largely true. In the 1940s, the advertising industry figured out how to market specific products to specific audiences. Record companies developed formulae for hit songs. Joseph Campbell's hero's journey codifies an ancient algorithm for storytelling so engaging that it has been used extensively in books, shows, and movies. All of these mechanisms for attracting attention have been enormously successful. However, the vast majority of attempts at compelling advertising or engaging music fail. Most film and television is mediocre, and viewers are anything but helplessly captivated or controlled. Plenty of people are turned off by formulaic stories or pop songs. A successful movie need only appeal to a small fraction of the population to smash at the box office, even if the majority is repulsed by it.

Those who worry about the algorithms used by today's tech companies need to tell us how their algorithms are fundamentally different from all of these prior advances in persuasion. Tech's critics like to say it's the sheer number of users, or the precision of the fine-tuning, or that it's embedded in our devices, or that the algorithms are designed from psychological research. But the question remains: At what point do any of these features suddenly take control of our minds and actions?

In its heyday, television advertising had enormous scale, and they used Nielsen ratings to effectively fine-tune their messaging. Advertising companies pioneered the use of focus groups and surveys, which essentially takes the form of psychological research. As a result, many people worried that this would doom civilization by placing viewers' minds into the hands of advertising and media firms. They were wrong. Today, the tech is different, but the critics' argument is the same—and just as wrong.

The truth is that these companies can't control us simply by knowing what we want, any more than television or print advertising can. We aren't passively controlled by our information diet—we make choices based on our interpretation of it. Most advertising doesn't work, and the ads that do work do so by telling us things about products that are true. False advertising fails in the long run because people get disappointed in the product, and the brand suffers as a result. Successful companies supply exaggerated but mostly true information about their products. The same is true with tech algorithms—they have to be mostly true in order to work.

Recent technological progress in this area is cause for optimism, because algorithms can increasingly give us what we want as *individuals*. Previously, most consumer products were produced for a mass audience with few options to customize for individual purposes. To get something custom-made is typically expensive. Smartphones and tablets are massive steps forward because, for the first time, we have high-quality products that can be customized to suit a range of personal needs. In some ways, the algorithms employed by tech platforms simply fine-tune customization, helping social media users find the people they are most interested in, shoppers find the products they want to buy, and music/television/movie viewers find the content they most want to consume.

This is an extraordinary opportunity that we should be careful not to demonize just because it's unprecedented. Don't let the Greedy Child Fallacy catch you—there's nothing wrong with getting what you want. If you want to engage with the most interesting people and content on the internet, a social media app just might be your thing, and there's nothing wrong with that.

WHAT ABOUT HARMFUL CONTENT?

It is impossible to ensure that kids never encounter harmful content without imposing totalitarian levels of surveillance and control. Furthermore, there's no way to force kids away from harmful content that doesn't risk generating a pathological interest in that content. As a gatekeeper, the only thing you can guarantee is that, when they find such content, they'll be careful to hide it from your disapproving eyes. And if they're confused or troubled by what they find, they won't seek guidance from a parent, they'll seek it from people who don't necessarily have their best interests at heart.

A trusted, knowledgeable, and approachable parent is a crucial safety mechanism for dealing with nasty stuff online. My kids regularly show me what they're watching, so I see everything that comes across their screens. They ask me questions about anything new, they tell me about what disturbs them, and since I have never taken their tablets away from them or expressed disapproval of what they see or do, they have no reason to hide anything from me.

Of course, there's more to worry about than just harmful *content*, because screens are portals to other *people*. Parents are rightly concerned about malicious adults, or cyberbullying from other kids who might shame, threaten, or blackmail their child by, for instance, sharing revealing photos. My first response is to note that, if my kids are open with me, then I will likely notice an online relationship with an adult stranger. As far as cyberbullying goes, I wonder if this is likely or even possible outside of compulsory schooling. When kids are forced into contact with bullies and hostile peers, this sets the stage for torments that can migrate online. And as for malicious adults, the best option might just be to help kids have trusting relationships among friends and family so they don't have reason to engage with creeps online.

In the end, there are many ways bad things can happen, but there's also no way to ensure that they won't. One of the few things we can control is how open and trustworthy we are with our kids as they navigate the culture. Personally, my biggest fear for my kids is that a screen-restricted friend of theirs, one who is forbidden from, and hence titillated by, the darker corners of the internet, will reveal it to them in secret. My best defense is that, hopefully, they'll want to tell me about it.

WHAT ABOUT SLEEP?

Our kids have unfettered access to their own iPads. The six-year-old goes to bed at around eight and leaves her tablet downstairs, preferring to be read to before dozing off. Her tablet has no discernible impact on her sleep. The three-year-old falls asleep at roughly the same time, sometimes joining her sister with a story the old-fashioned way, and sometimes staying up an extra hour watching *Peppa Pig*. I'd say that, on an average week, she stays awake three hours longer than she would if she didn't have a tablet. My five-year-old, on the other hand, loves his tablet and stays up several hours later than he would otherwise, sometimes close to midnight. When he was three and four, he would compensate with long naps in the afternoon, but now these have tapered off, and he generally falls asleep between nine and ten.

Even though they often stay up later because of screens, I don't think screens disrupt their sleep because they don't have to wake up early in the morning. As I described in Chapter Two, if kids are missing sleep because they're forced to wake up for school, then school is the culprit. Overall, I'd guess my kids get as much sleep as other kids their age, and they don't appear particularly tired during the day. Occasionally my son's late nights are disruptive to my wife and me. He might ask for some food or want to show us the funny thing he just saw. However, these are well worth the utter absence of tension and pressure at night. Some nights I do worry that the screens are keeping them up too late and messing with their sleep rhythms, but when I consider the heavy costs of using boredom as a deliberate tool to get them to sleep, I relax and drift off.

WHAT ABOUT THE EYES?

Some are concerned that screens are harmful to visual acuity, causing kids to need glasses. Even if these claims are valid, I've heard the same said about books, yet I've never heard anyone seriously suggest that reading should be limited to spare the eyes. I think using screens is at least as important as reading, perhaps more so in the modern age. If this causes some injury to young people's vision, I think that's worth addressing, but it is not in itself justification for limiting screens, especially when we have no idea how much we'd need to limit in order to preserve vision.

Blue light is another concern. The worry here is that blue light suppresses melatonin, which is essential for sleep. Whether or not this is true is irrelevant, because modern screens can automatically correct their output based on the ambient light. This might seem like a throwaway point, but there is something deeper at play. As technology improves, various safetyist arguments for restrictions lose their punch. But those restrictions, once in place, can last well past the time that they'd already become moot. This is yet another reason to be optimistic about the massive scale of this industry; it makes economic sense for the manufacturers to improve their products.

ISN'T BOREDOM GOOD?

Boredom is bad for the same reasons pain is bad. Both indicate suffering. Both indicate a problem that needs solving. And neither is a virtue in its own right. We wouldn't arbitrarily expose a child to pain with the argument that pain is an inevitable part of life that they need to "learn to deal with." Such cruelty teaches children that, not only are we indifferent to their suffering, but they should accept their suffering as well. Instead, when a child comes to us in pain, we always investigate why, partly for our own peace of mind, but also to give the child context to understand the pain. When we ourselves understand that the injury is minor, we explain to the child that it will heal, and this understanding is soothing. And of course we take a few steps to mitigate the pain and prevent it from happening again.

We should apply the same basic process for all suffering, including boredom. All suffering is caused by some form of ignorance, and it can be mitigated and outright prevented by some form of knowledge. All of parenting can be summarized as supplying the child with the knowledge to reduce their own suffering.

Valorizing boredom is the other half of the Greedy Child Fallacy. If, according to the fallacy, getting what you want is bad, then being in a state of discomfort is good. This is completely backward. We admire people who endure great discomfort when that discomfort is essential to satisfying their passions, but we call people who endure discomfort just to demonstrate their toughness derogatory names like "meatheads." Toughness and grit are virtuous when there's a *reason* to be tough and gritty. We want our kids to be passionate, to have such strong reasons for doing what they want that they are willing to endure temporary hardships to get there. We'd also like them to take a minute and try to minimize the hardships.

CONCLUSION

Mobile computing is new, and we're trying to figure out how to use it. It's naive to think all of the disruptions caused by mobile devices are an unalloyed good. It is perfectly reasonable to worry about damage to traditional institutions and norms before we have improved options to replace them with, and this is especially true when it comes to children. But it is not reasonable to be alarmist about these changes, which is an all-too-easy option to get publicity, social clout, or funding for a research program. It is not reasonable to assume that anything new is bad. It is not reasonable to misuse concepts like addiction or brain chemistry to drive fear. And in the context of disruption, it is not right to invoke the necessity of control.

Conventional parenting assumes not just a right but a duty to control kids' attention. Like with food, the general worry is that, if left to their own devices, kids will indulge in cheap, superficial "junk" content that will melt their minds. This misconception runs against the reality that kids have a powerful desire to explore, discover, and learn. Exploration *requires* autonomy over one's own attention. Extinguish this autonomy, and creative exploration is replaced with apathy and a willingness to settle for what's immediately available. The desire to explore doesn't turn off when children pick up a screen. Instead, their options expand more than with any other household object.

Today's screens are extraordinary because they bring nearly anything digitizable into one place. They are stories, games, movies, TV series, search, humor, language, socializing, art, and knowledge of all stripes. But for many adults, their perspective is of a kid staring vacantly at a flat surface.

Homogenizing this stimulating and dynamic medley into one thing—one *bad* thing—called "screen time" is a farce. Limiting screens does not open kids up to the outside world; it closes them off from it. It deprives kids of a safe, low-cost avenue through which to sample the world on their own terms, from the comfort and convenience of a couch or the back seat of a car. Screens are one of the most unambiguously useful things in life, for adults and kids. If we deprive kids of these crucial cultural tools, we deny them one of the most dynamic portals to discovery that humanity has ever created.

Chapter Four

THE FOUR PROBLEMS WITH RULES

MY GOAL IN THIS CHAPTER IS TO SHOW THAT ENFORCING rules on children produces so many problems that you'll become interested in seeking an alternative. Rules-based parenting always damages children's relationship with their parents and with themselves, and it introduces deep and persistent confusions about the world.

To be sure, the arguments *for* imposing rules sound reasonable on their face. After all, children come into this world utterly ignorant about what's in their best interest. Therefore, so the argument goes, an authority figure needs to prevent them from doing things whose harmful effects will only be felt later on, such as unhealthy eating and sleeping habits, antisocial behavior patterns, and addictive pastimes such as anything to do with screens. In short, parents have a responsibility to control their children's decisions that could, if left to the kids' own devices, result in long-term mental, physical, or emotional underdevelopment and pathology. These days, this kind of argument often comes with a caveat—parents shouldn't *overdo* enforcing the rules necessary to ward off all of these long-term risks, but sometimes duty calls for them to put their foot down and be tough.

In addition to the argument that enforcing rules is in the child's best interest, the vast majority of people today accept a false dichotomy—that the absence of rule enforcement amounts to child neglect. As we've already seen, there is a third option, one that requires neither arbitrary control of the child nor immoral neglect from the parents.

Yet another argument in favor of rule enforcement is that, despite their protestations, kids actually *want* structure. They want to know where the boundaries are so they can relax and operate freely within them. So long as you explain why you're enforcing rules and apply them consistently, the child will typically be grateful and will flourish within the bounds you've set. And if there is any short-term suffering due to your enforced rules, this is unfortunate but unavoidable collateral damage in the service of kids' long-term interests. Critically, even *if* a kid fails to appreciate your rules during their childhood, *they will certainly come to appreciate them when they grow up.*

As a former schoolteacher and coach, I once found this approach to be reasonable and effective. Now, as a parent, I've realized that the resultant damage of enforcing rules for my kids and my relationship with them is so serious and long-lasting that it's worth investigating an alternative.

A NOTE ON TERMINOLOGY

The word *rule* means different things for adults and children, because kids generally can't opt out of rules.

Adults can almost always opt out of rules. They always have the option to leave almost any situation and go to the privacy of their home, where even the police can't enter without a special dispensation. In fact, rules that adults can't opt out of aren't called rules, they're called laws.

Kids, on the other hand, can rarely opt out. Rules for kids almost always entail force. Even if force isn't applied, the mere threat of it is enough. In the absence of force, a kid may be made to feel so uncomfortable, either through shaming or deprivation of privileges, that they are essentially forced psychologically. And since kids are dependent on their parents, they can't escape.

Not all of the rules in a kid's life are obligatory, such as the rules of a game. The rules of chess or baseball are special because they have been found to be so much fun that children comply with them *voluntarily*, and that makes all the difference. Everyone can opt out, but they willingly engage because these rules solve problems for all parties.

One last type of beneficial rule is a boundary. Boundaries are rules or limitations that people voluntarily impose on themselves. When I set a boundary on myself, I am declaring how much of my own space, time, and resources I'm willing to offer others. The nice thing about boundaries is that other people, including kids, can opt out of them.

Of course, parents are in a unique situation in that there are certain boundaries that they cannot enforce with their kids. They cannot declare, for example, that they aren't providing food or clothing for their kids. But they absolutely can declare that they aren't spending all of their money on candy and toys.

As a shorthand, all references to rules in this book refer to rules that kids can't opt out of. This book is not opposed to rules. On the contrary, systems of rules that attract willing participants, such as the rules of grammar or conventions of courtesy, also known as institutions, are among the most important of human discoveries. In fact, a major problem with enforcing arbitrary rules is the damage this does to a child's engagement with our greatest institutions.

FIRST FOUL: THE
PARENT–CHILD RELATIONSHIP

Rule enforcement damages the relationship between parent and child in several ways. When you, the parent, are enforcing limits on food, on staying up, or on using screens, you become the gatekeeper to these things. And gatekeepers are always obstacles to be opposed and outmaneuvered. Since food and screens and sleep play a role in everyone's daily life, this gate-keeping is a constant job, which puts kids in a continual state of opposition. The old-school way of avoiding the painstaking work of gatekeeping was to be threatening and intimidating. "Don't even ask," the parent might say in clipped tones. The simple act of asking *why* the gate to this or that must be kept closed was considered punishable defiance, and so the child kept their mouth shut due to fear alone.

When faced with a gatekeeper, the creative mind can't help but think of ways around this barrier. "Maybe I'll sneak the cookie when she's not looking. Maybe I'll lie. Maybe I'll find a different adult who will do it for me. Maybe I can make her feel guilty about something and give in. Or maybe I can just wear her down by asking." Even if the issue in question seems trivial, the more often the kid engages with the thing being gatekept, the more often they will think thoughts like this. You simply cannot limit things that kids want without giving them reasons to at least consider becoming manipulative and deceptive.

I've seen parents bemoan how deceptive even small children can be, while ignoring the fact that they're the ones who gave the kid a reason to deceive in the first place. I've heard parents describe children as being deceitful by nature, as if they're born not knowing how to talk but with the knowledge of how to deceive. In fact, deceit is a perfectly rational way to get around a barrier—especially one erected for no apparent reason.

I myself have weaseled around many rules in my adult life, and nothing motivates me more than a rule that doesn't make sense. I am much more inclined to follow a rule when I know the reason for it, even if I disagree with it. But given their youthful ignorance, children rarely come to understand the reason for the rule on their own, even when explained, because it is not often that an adult can put an abstract concept into words in such a way that a child can understand. So, not only do most rules seem meaningless and arbitrary to a child, some appear specifically designed just to thwart and punish them.

A common example of this is when sweets are left out on a table, often during a party or family gathering, but kids are told they can have just one. Meanwhile, adults can eat as many as they want, since we don't issue rules for how many cookies the adults in the room can take. There couldn't be a more blatant double standard.

When an enterprising kid hatches a plan to sneak a second cookie, they get accused of being deceitful—not just deceitful in that moment, but deceitful in their bones, in their very nature. Things can spiral out of control if parents use this mistaken idea to proclaim the need to enforce rules even *more* thoroughly in order to bend the deceitful nature of these children into rectitude. And so it goes in a vicious cycle, either until the kid gives up—which entails snuffing out a part of their own creativity and interests—or until they're old enough that the parents relax their strictures.

But in this instance the prognosis of inherent deceitfulness is utterly wrongheaded. The child has been given a perfectly good reason to be deceptive in the face of the cookie double standard. Deceit is not in their nature, but it is cultivated by arbitrary, unexplained, unreasonable rules.

Kids' minds (just like those of adults) are constantly running, cooking up theories of what's going on. When this theorizing arrives at an explanation that seems to make sense of their surroundings, such as that "the adults who put cookies out that I can't have are my adversaries," then they will operate in accordance with that theory. As a parent, you won't necessarily be able to tell what ideas your child is acting on. Like them, you'll have to guess. But the child may become skilled at deflecting your suspicions. For instance, the child may guess that it's best to tell parents what they want to hear rather than what the child truly thinks. As our cookie example shows, enforcing a rule about how many cookies is too many cookies triggers the child to conjure up a cascade of theories for how to deal with you. When eying the plate of cookies, the child is learning how to *overcome* you, the enforcer.

No wonder that parents of even small children say in exasperation, "I don't know what her problem is!" A big reason you don't know is that you have created an environment in which the child has every reason to use their incredible powers of learning to try to foil your gatekeeping by keeping you in the dark. If a toddler can learn a language, they can surely learn some strategies for getting what they want.

When limits are enforced, parents become just that— enforcers. It's bad enough to be a gatekeeper, but *enforcers* issue *consequences*. Recall that the child doesn't understand why rules are there in the first place. No amount of enforcement, no amount of terrifying, *imposed* consequences can possibly help a child understand the purpose of a rule.

"I've told you a thousand times!" the parent barks at the child. Yes, which means they don't understand. When kids don't understand a rule, they don't sit back in awe of the magisterial power of the rule maker. Instead, they develop psychological coping mechanisms such as resentment, fearfulness, rebelliousness, confusion, or apathy.

Nietzsche based an entire philosophy on resentment because it is such a powerful and self-defining emotion. Resentment can boil over as outright hostility or defensiveness, but its real danger is that it can simmer under the surface, constantly stoked by blocks and denials from parents. Resentment drives people to blame others for their unhappiness or inability to achieve their goals, which helps to establish an external locus of control and a forfeiting of autonomy. A resentful child might get in the habit of looking for others to blame as the reason for their troubles. We've met these people as adults, and it's harder to think of a more damaging way to be in the world. In fact, our chief job as parents may be to help our children develop an internal locus of control, to feel like they are responsible for their destiny, and that it is their job to figure out how to interact productively with others and the world at large.

I'm not saying that enforcing rules always engenders resentment and learned helplessness. I'm saying it's a marvel that kids so often overcome this.

A gatekeeper and enforcer needs a judge, someone to decide when a rule has been breached or when a new rule needs to be applied, or when extenuating circumstances warrant pausing the rule. Can kids eat more sweets on vacation? Can they watch screens longer than usual when at a friend's house? Surely the children don't get to make these decisions, so the parent is the judge. Adding the role of judge gives children even more reason to deceive. When a kid goes to a friend's house and the rules are looser, how can a kid not think to hide this fact from the parent-judge?

Rules-based parenting also requires surveillance, which means the parent needs to keep an eye out at all times. From the child's perspective, this means that they can never fully relax. Even if there is no *need* to enforce a rule, the mere presence of an arbitrary enforcer implies that the hammer *could* drop on any activity at any moment. Under such a capricious and omnipresent threat, it's perfectly reasonable for a child to develop a constant psychological backdrop of alertness and anxiety.

Think about what it's like to work in the direct presence of your boss. Even if they don't say anything, you are slightly on edge, because you have to police yourself so that you don't step out of line. The range of acceptable things to do has narrowed, and part of you needs to pay attention to your impulses so that you don't break a rule. This paying attention is what it means to be self-conscious and is an essential ingredient in anxiety and low self-esteem.

But this self-consciousness can be even worse for kids. When you are in the presence of your boss, at least you know *why* there is a boss and what is and is not acceptable behavior at work. You also have the opportunity to leave and get a new job with a more relaxed boss, so the stakes are not quite so high.

But kids are ignorant—they don't understand how the rules work, so for them, the presence of an enforcer will feel more arbitrary. When a toddler climbs up on a table, they have no idea that "There's no climbing on tables." This rule comes at them from out of the blue, which means that, from their vantage point, another rule might come out of the blue at any other time. They never know if the next thing they do might also be considered wrong. Again, even if the rule is not arbitrary from the parent's point of view—for instance, if the table is a dangerous place for a toddler—the rule is perceived as arbitrary to the child. How could they see it otherwise?

I'm not saying parents should leave toddlers to climb on tables. I'm saying there shouldn't be a *rule* that there's no climbing on tables. Instead, figure out how to make the table safe. Find something else for the kid to climb on. If you really don't want them on the table, keep the chairs away. I'll have a lot more to say about alternatives to rules elsewhere, but for now, I'm only saying that neglect is not a viable alternative to rules.

Another casualty of rule enforcement is trust. That's because surveillance is the opposite of trust. We don't completely trust people who are watching over us, ever ready to block us from stuff that we want. If a kid has been given a reason to dream up ideas for how to get around you as a gatekeeper, and if those ideas are hardened by resentment and have manifested as this or that scheme, then there is no way they are going to reveal that scheme to you. They're not going to talk about the fear or anxiety they feel about you finding out. They're not going to tell you about their strategy for getting past you, nor their moral deliberations about the lie they have cooked up. They might share this with their siblings or friends, but not with you.

Kids may trust their parents in specific domains, such as physical safety, and this is of course crucial. But there is an enormous difference between partial and total trust. If kids don't trust their parents completely, then that means there are some issues where kids will seek guidance from someone else. Therefore, rules—contrary to their stated purpose—do *not* keep kids safe, disciplined, or healthy. Rather, they drive kids to other people who are less committed to their well-being.

They may seek advice and support from their friends or some wise-seeming grown-up, such as an older kid in school or someone on the internet. They may develop an alternate persona such that they show one face to their parents and a different, more genuine face to those who don't try to control them. How many movies and TV shows about kids hinge on this dual persona that kids use around parents and teachers? In these stories, it isn't at all surprising to viewers that the parents are portrayed as oblivious to the real goings-on among the kids. In fact, this obliviousness is part of the charm.

When a kid adopts a persona, they create a whole life about which the parent is largely in the dark, and the kid becomes adept at keeping it this way so as to escape the surveillance, gatekeeping, and enforcement that hold sway in adult-land.

The recognition that severe rule enforcement can backfire and lead kids to seek out the very activities that were prohibited seems to have seeped into the culture, which is good. However, the strategy for avoiding this backfiring seems not to be the large-scale reduction or elimination of rules. Instead, the rise of overprotective parenting has brought about many new rules, and it has also increased surveillance. Helicopter parents do more policing and enforce more limitations today than in previous, more strict generations.

Modern parenting tries to soften rule enforcement, to not be so hard-nosed. When cookies are denied, a parent might explain the health problems with cookies rather than saying "because I said so" in a stern, disapproving tone. While this comes from a good place—the desire to not drive kids to resent their parents—it replaces the overt coercion of the parents of yesteryear, such as spanking, with more manipulative forms of rule enforcement, such as shaming kids for wanting something. The child's interests are still thwarted, but it's less obvious that the parent is the cause. Instead, the child has reason to shift the blame *inward*, to think their desire to eat the cookie comes from their inherent unhealthiness, which brings us to the next major category of harm.

SECOND FOUL: RELATIONSHIP WITH SELF

Every time a kid has a rule forced on them, it carries with it a negative message about who they are as a person, and this gives the kid a reason to doubt themself. Put differently, there is no way to enforce a rule on a child and guarantee that the child won't take it personally in some way. To illustrate, let's compare the difference between rule enforcement for adults, like when they get a parking ticket, versus kids, like when they're made to brush their teeth.

The first difference is that when an adult gets a parking ticket, the attendant doesn't scold the driver. The ticket is applied and resolved dispassionately. This is possible because adults have knowledge about *why* there are rules for parking, what the specific rules are, and how to resolve instances of breaking them. Adults know that parking rules apply to everyone equally, and that there's nothing personal about receiving a parking ticket.

In contrast, children *are* often scolded for not brushing their teeth. Even if parents don't scold, they tend to use language that conveys their annoyance or disappointment at having to force the issue. It is extremely hard to force a kid to do something while remaining dispassionate. Even being robotic about it can cause them to take offense. When I've done this, my daughter has complained that I'm being distant and that she feels slighted. When forced to brush their teeth, kids have their guard up and are predisposed to take offense because they don't understand the underlying *why*. They may be able to parrot back some words about keeping their teeth healthy, but they don't really know what that means. They don't know what a root canal feels like, or the delight of a winning smile, or the hassle of dentures.

Children don't understand teeth the way adults understand parking and traffic. And, given their ignorance, children don't know that the teeth brushing rule isn't about them personally, that the reasons for brushing teeth apply equally to everyone with teeth. In their ignorance, kids are prone to think the rules are arbitrary and designed to penalize and persecute them.

Second, adults know how to resolve a parking ticket and restore their status before the law. Kids, on the other hand, might be unsure of whether or how to redeem themselves, and instead see the enforcement as a penalty that they are left to ruminate over.

Third, adults can opt out of the rules of parking. They can decide to ride a bike or walk or just stay home. But kids can't opt out of a teeth-brushing rule. When it's time for bed, their mom or dad will hunt them down, disrupt whatever they are doing, and make the brushing happen.

And finally, in the adult's world, the parking attendant, judge, fine enforcer, and lawmaker are all different people, each serving as a check on the others. This individuation of roles also depersonalizes the issue by making the entire process publicly accountable and objective. In modern families, kids might be able to appeal the teeth-brushing rule and be granted a conversation. They might even be encouraged to question the rules. But in the end, they are brushing their teeth—end of story. And, since judge, jury, and executioner are all rolled into one, the door is open to all of the problems of kangaroo courts—hasty, ad hoc decisions lacking even the appearance of objectivity.

This example shows several reasons kids have for taking rules personally, for assuming it says something about them as a person, about their character or their self-worth. If I want a thing, but getting that thing is bad, then something about *me* must be bad. If some essential part of me is bad, then following my desires can get me into trouble. This means my own desires, my gut intuitions, are not to be trusted. And not trusting oneself is the heart of self-doubt and insecurity. Hence, the second Foul of rules is their damage to kids' relationship with themselves.

Might lifelong habits of insecurity get formed in childhood? When kids are continuously thwarted regarding things as basic as eating and sleeping, coming and going, and paying attention to this or that, do some of them become adults who mistrust and war with themselves? See Chapter Ten for more on the consequences of mistaken ideas about human nature.

Emotions and Self-Doubt

Over time, parents have generally relaxed the severity of rule enforcement. Corporal punishment is stigmatized, parents recoil at the idea that children should be seen and not heard, and parents increasingly value freedom and autonomy. But since rules are still understood to be a necessary evil, strategies have emerged that preserve rules by making their enforcement more gentle. While this strategy is well-meaning, it risks convincing kids that their own emotions are the enemy, and this sets the stage for warring with oneself.

For instance, one popular strategy for softening rules is to "help" kids control their emotions. The idea here is that the real problem with rule enforcement is the kids' expression of anger or unhappiness. If only kids didn't act out their anger, then the system of rules would work swimmingly. To that end, parents and teachers counsel kids on how to control or regulate their anger. After all, adults rarely scream and shout when they don't get what they want. The sooner kids learn to copy this behavior, so the thinking goes, the better off everyone would be.

A parent counseling anger control for their child often sounds something like this: "You are feeling angry at being told it's time to go, and that is natural. Take some deep breaths, relax, and let it pass." Besides breathing, kids are offered several methods for controlling their emotions, such as counting to ten, punching pillows, or meditating.

What's wrong with this? It confuses emotional *regulation* with emotional *mastery*. It recommends suppressing or ignoring emotions rather than developing and using them effectively.

Take a mature adult who is mistreated at work. Adults know not to throw themselves on the floor and scream, because they know that doing so would make it *harder* to get what they want, which is for their coworker to stop mistreating them. Instead, the adult might play it cool and show no outward signs of offense so as to appear professional and trustworthy when complaining to the boss. Submitting a carefully worded complaint is a much better and more effective way to be angry than throwing a tantrum.

Mature adults don't just suppress their anger. They don't just accept or ignore the causes of anger. Instead, they choose to direct it in a way that they have learned will get them what they want. In fact, it is easy to keep your cool when you know how to correct the underlying injustice. Even if you're unsure how to make the injustice right, merely having confidence in your ability to figure it out is often enough to steady one's nerves and focus on a solution.

It is therefore counterproductive to teach kids that anger is something to be suppressed. Unfortunately, emotions tend to be treated as storms of feelings that well up from some unknowable region inside of us. It's thought that they need to be either contained or diverted, lest these feelings disturb others or embarrass us. This theory leaves kids with the self-injurious idea that emotions have no real purpose, that they just muck up our thinking, that they make us say and do irrational, harmful things, and hence present a constant threat to our image and comportment.

In reality, emotions bubble up for *reasons;* they are always *about* something. We feel grief *about* a loss, fear *about* a threat, and anger *about* being wronged. If a kid gets angry, it is a disservice to ignore the object of their anger and instead try to lessen or neutralize the angry feelings. In reality, resolving anger is about resolving the injustice in the eyes of the aggrieved, not taking deep breaths or taking the feeling out on a punching bag.

But training kids to suppress their anger without helping them correct its cause does precisely the opposite—it signals that understanding the underlying problem is irrelevant. They're essentially taught that they need to brush their teeth whether they like it or not, whether they understand or not, and that bursting out in anger is not appropriate. It's a double insult—forced to brush *and* forced to be quiet about it. This reduces their confidence in themselves as a corrector of wrongs. Trying to mollify an angry person by telling them to breathe is a refusal to take them seriously. To take anger seriously is to inquire about the underlying problem and help the person solve it by their own lights.

Emotions are good. In fact, they are among the best and most enriching things in life. Teaching kids to doubt or suppress or be ashamed of their emotions is potentially catastrophic. To be sure, this doesn't mean we leave kids to exercise their anger any way they want, as that would be neglect. Instead, we help kids address the actual object of their anger (or sadness, or nervousness, or any other emotion) authentically. We support their efforts to resolve it and learn how to express their emotions in a way that is consistent with finding a resolution.

We opened this section discussing desires—they are good, too. It is possible to help a kid genuinely engage with any desire in a way that isn't dangerous. In fact, this is much of what becoming an adult is—expressing emotions and pursuing desires in productive ways.

THIRD FOUL: CONFUSION
ABOUT THE PROBLEM

Rules and limits are often enforced to "make kids understand" certain hard truths about the world, such as that you can't always get what you want, or that life isn't fair. In reality, rule enforcement can't teach about the world. As we've already seen, the enforcement of rules and limitations diverts the focus away from the problem itself and toward the parent and whatever contrived consequences the parent is willing to impose. Rules are *confusing*.

Take the teeth-brushing example again. Forcing a kid to brush their teeth directs the kid's attention away from the benefits of brushing teeth and focuses it on the consequences of not brushing. A kid might simply comply, but like all rules, the rule enforcement might backfire. If a kid decides to have a standoff with Mom or Dad, then brushing teeth is really about fighting with one's parents. This is such a common occurrence that there is a lot of parenting advice about how to make your kid brush their teeth without battles.

Even if a kid complies with the teeth-brushing rule, if they do it under threat of force, then their reason for doing it was to avoid the consequences of force, not because they understood the benefits of teeth brushing.

One might think the solution here is to simply explain what the rule is for. I agree, but with some critical reservations. The first is that an explanation often doesn't work, especially for small children. Parents often reward themselves for being reasonable because they "had that conversation" with their kid, but in reality the conversation really amounts to a talking-to. A lecture is almost never wanted, and kids tend to comply just to get the lecture over with. Yes, sometimes you can communicate effective explanations to small children, and that is a terrific success. But it's important to reflect on whether the goal is really achieved, and one way of testing that is to see if the kid does it (whatever it is) voluntarily after you've offered your explanation.

This is the key: doing something without the presence of enforcement or threats thereof is one of the best indicators that a person has a good understanding of what that thing is for. By forcing things, the parent is virtually guaranteeing that they can't possibly determine whether or not their kid understands. In fact, forcing the kid to act under duress only hinders their ability to understand *why* the thing is worth doing in the first place.

If something is so important that it's worth incurring relationship damage to get a kid to do it, then it's even more important that the kid understands why that thing is necessary. When kids grow up, all they will have to rely on when navigating the risks and pitfalls in the world is their own understanding and their relationships with people who have experience and knowledge. Forcing kids to comply with rules about these important things disrupts their developing understanding of these things.

A related example is the confusing effects of forcing kids to be courteous and polite. Conveying gratitude, appreciation, and regret requires lots of nuance, just the right words at just the right time, with just the right tone of voice and body language.

In order to get it right, a learner must be in tune with the other person, paying close attention to how they react and adjusting accordingly. But if politeness and consideration are instead made to be about parental expectations, this distracts from the authentic engagement with others that is necessary to learn the relevant nuances. If a child is simply told to act polite or say they're sorry, then their learning might stop once they have muttered the magic words and gotten their parents off their back. Gratitude, with all of its emotional richness, gets replaced with an authoritarian "Say thank you" and its accompanying tit-for-tat emotional sterility.

When a toddler receives a gift, it's common to see their eyes light up with a genuine feeling of gratitude, see it radiate from their whole body, and then witness it get stamped out when a parent says, "Well, what do you say?" This interjection, which is intended to teach gratitude, in fact turns genuine gratitude into shame, often public shame when it occurs at a party or family gathering. While at first the kid was rejoicing, they now feel like they did something wrong. They stare at the floor, sheepishly force out a "thank you," and then run off to play in the absence of both the politeness police and the gift giver. Forced gratitude is nothing like actual gratitude, and the result is emotional confusion instead of mastery. "Teaching kids to show respect" can disrupt actually learning to show respect.

You might worry that if kids are left to their own devices, they won't develop crucial life skills, like manners, norms around communication, and etiquette. But because those things are so fundamental, the child will inevitably want to learn them because it will help them pursue their interests. For instance, if your kid is interested in telling jokes, they'll have to learn how to capture someone else's attention pursuant to this goal. And *that* entails persuasion, which in turn requires loads of knowledge around social norms. They might not care about manners and etiquette per se, but when they realize that such skills help them land an audience for their joke telling, they'll learn manners and etiquette without reservation.

Similarly, so long as their pursuits require interpersonal interactions, they will want their apologies to land sincerely and effectively, and they will want those who give them gifts and do them favors to know that their generosity is appreciated. They will also want their teeth to look and feel good. They will want to live in a household where boundaries are respected and not chaotic. And so it goes for all of the things we consider essential for kids to learn. If these essential things are truly essential, then they are useful, and kids will learn them in order to get what they want out of the world.

And for all of these things, they will figure out how to do it the same way they figured out other complicated and important things, like learning how to talk—by trying out different approaches and sticking with what works. Parents can help by explaining to and showing kids how things work and offering tips, but perhaps the most important contribution is to avoid disrupting this process by diverting attention away from their native interests via rule enforcement.

FOURTH FOUL: CONFUSION ABOUT HOW TO SOLVE PROBLEMS

In the real world, there are no ultimate authorities on what is right and wrong. Nobody knows for sure how many hours of sleep we should get or what the ideal diet is. When confronted with a problem, there is no person who definitely has the answer. Instead, we are on our own, left to figure out for ourselves what is the best way forward. People and knowledge are available to help, but no one is infallible, and it is up to us to determine who to listen to and what information is reliable. In the adult world, we solve our own problems. From the most trivial to the most consequential, we are the authors of our own lives, or at least we aspire to be.

Given this aspiration, it's hard to think of a more important gift to give our children than the confidence to be the authors of their own lives, to acquire the knowledge, skills, and assertiveness to take ownership of their own affairs. And this reveals the fourth Foul of enforcing rules—it confuses kids by teaching them that there are external authorities who know the answers about how to live. It teaches them that, when their interests conflict with those around them, the answer is to find the proper authority and do what they say, rather than to resolve the conflict themselves. It subverts their own autonomy and orients them to an external locus of control.

Here, I'm using the word *authority* to refer to someone with purportedly definitive knowledge, what we informally call "an authority on the subject." This is a conventional usage, but philosophically it is nonsensical. No one has final, confirmed, unalterable knowledge on any subject.

The word *authority* can also refer to a person vested, or authorized, with certain powers. This kind of authority is very real, and parents have this property as well. They are vested with legal powers as well as physical power over their kids. I'm not denying this at all. I am saying that children should be spared the nonsensical idea that parents have ultimate knowledge, but not the very real idea that their parents have certain powers.

The goal is for children to be free of limitations set upon them by external "authorities" of knowledge. But that's not to say we pretend they are totally free from constraints. We want them to operate within the constraints of the natural world.

Indeed, they have no choice but to accept gravity and the hardness of concrete. And we want them to operate within some of the constraints of the interpersonal world.

Specifically, there are two kinds of good interpersonal constraints:

1. Other people's boundaries. We don't want kids to think they can demand anything they want from others.
2. Constraints that they accept voluntarily, such as the rules of a game or conventions of politeness.

In general, we want kids to understand the natural world, to respect other people's boundaries, and to accept the interpersonal constraints they understand, and reject those that they don't. This voluntary engagement helps ensure that their knowledge grows organically, genuinely, under their own control, and with minimal distortion and confusion by arbitrary and contrived rules.

For the most part, our culture celebrates autonomy, self-assertion, and a can-do attitude. Yet kids are raised to deny, suppress, and control this instinct. Most modern parents know the value of modeling the behaviors they want to see in the world, but they often model authoritarianism and conformity by making kids stick to limits that they don't understand and that are chosen by purportedly all-knowing parents. We raise kids in a kind of training environment where they need to conform to authorities, and then we release them into the world hoping that they suddenly make the mental pivot to figuring things out for themselves.

I'm not saying we should leave children entirely on their own, to figure things out with no parental input. I'm saying there is a way to help people without impairing their agency.

We do this with friends and adult family all the time, offering guidance when it's asked for and even stepping in aggressively, albeit rarely, when we see impending disaster. And I'm not saying it's easy or that we should expect 100 percent success in safely preserving our kids' autonomy. I'm saying it is an achievable ideal worth striving for, not just in select areas but in every domain of life. And when preserving autonomy is a top priority, not only can we get quite good at it, but our kids become more open to trusting our input. When they know we are not trying to take control and demote them to a minor role in their own lives, they are more open to our suggestions.

CONCLUSION: THE FOUL FOUR
ARE UNAVOIDABLE

If rules are as bad as I've said, why don't more people point to the rule-induced scars from their childhood?

Fortunately, many people correct the mistakes that were made during their childhood and don't harbor resentment or insecurity as adults. This is a favorable outcome, but it is not guaranteed, and it still has some drawbacks. Even if the childhood anguish is eventually overcome, it still exacts a cost. The degraded relationships and confusions described by the Foul Four may be restored, but until that state of restoration is reached, children still suffer the consequences and lost opportunities of rule enforcement.

Another drawback is that adults whose rules-induced injuries have healed may nonetheless impose rules on their children. The common refrain that "I turned out alright" is not a good reason to impose the same conditions on someone else.

The remnants of the Foul Four in our adult lives often go unrecognized. Adults' relationships with their parents may remain marked by judgment, defensiveness, and a lack of respect for autonomy. Many adults have hang-ups about food and sleep and struggle with "unhealthy" relationships with various temptations. Many adults worry that they are a bad person. Many adults are consumed by the rules and expectations of life rather than with life itself.

Our culture sugarcoats and obfuscates the harmful effects of rule enforcement, thereby preserving the primary tool parents and schoolteachers use to manage kids. The need to preserve those tools gives rule enforcement a lot of positive press. Whenever I've heard the following phrases, they have always been issued in a boastful, self-congratulatory tone: "I straightened him out." "Time to set some ground rules." "She'll get over it." "You need to nip it in the bud." "It's for her own good." "He'll thank you when he's older." "I taught him a lesson."

Finally, the reasons kids have for doing what they do are invisible to parents. It is easy to have a false impression that a kid is complying because they agree with the rules, when in fact many kids learn to simply say what their parents want to hear—after all, if you're never going to win, why raise a stink about it? The same goes internally—it's no fun feeling hostile toward the people you love, and one way to resolve this is to convince yourself that the rules they impose on you make sense. Imagine if kids could speak correctly and honestly about their feelings and thoughts as they comply with our rules.

Chapter Five

PARENTING WITHOUT RULES

WHEN KIDS CAN'T OPT OUT OF RULES, IT CAN CAUSE such a wide range of serious and long-lasting harms that it's worth considering alternatives.

The alternative to rules that comes most readily to mind is free rein, letting kids do whatever they want. But that is just neglect. Parents are morally obligated to foster their kids' safety and well-being and guide them as they learn about the world.

The most popular option is to find a "balance" that expands freedom and autonomy but relies on a few "gentle but firm" rules as guardrails.

This is the predominant mode of modern parenting, a mixture of permissiveness and authoritarianism. The technical term is *authoritative*, and it is presented as a reasonable compromise between two extremes. In the words of the American Psychological Association, authoritative parents are "nurturing, responsive, and supportive, yet set firm limits for their children."

This compromise seems perfectly reasonable, but in fact it sets the stage for the eternal question of parenting—where do you draw the line? When is a "firm limit" also "responsive"? The very process of setting a limit means at some point you are not responding to the protests of your child (namely, when your child openly disagrees with the limit). If you are always responsive to protests, then the limit is a suggestion, and therefore not firm. On the other hand, even old-school authoritarian parents could claim to be "nurturing, responsive, and supportive" because they literally fed, clothed, and housed their children, often at great personal cost.

Some parenting strategies recognize that drawing lines is arbitrary and instead focus on concocting methods for making the line more palatable. Some try to promote freedom in one area but restrict it in others, such as allowing children to choose whatever clothes they want but not whatever food they want. The idea is that having an outlet for free expression will make a kid more docile in the face of limits in other areas of life. Other strategies give the appearance of promoting choice while controlling the range of available choices, such as offering three different foods as the only options for lunch. Some include soliciting input from the children about what the rules should be, as if choosing your limitations makes them voluntary.

So, if I'm arguing against rules, and I'm arguing against free rein, and I'm arguing against an irrational mixture of the two, what am I arguing *for*?

PROBLEM-SOLVING FROM THE
KID'S POINT OF VIEW

When the parent wants their kid to brush their teeth but the kid refuses, they both have a problem. Is there a way to solve this problem that works for the parent *and* the kid? In short, can we find a win–win solution? Fortunately, the answer is always *yes.* (Not only is there a win–win solution for every problem, but there is an *infinity* of them.)

One reason many parents find this optimistic stance inconceivable is precisely because they are adamant about sticking to rule enforcement as the "solution" and think that any non-enforced solution would only result in disaster. But once you drop the insistence that a solution must include enforcing rules, the space of possible win–win solutions becomes so much easier, more exciting, and fun to explore.

Let me walk you through how this works with the teeth-brushing example.

Why does a kid not want to brush their teeth? Maybe they don't like the taste of the toothpaste or the feel of the brush. The parent can try sampling different toothpastes and brushes. They could make a special trip to the store and let the kid pick out several varieties to take home and try out. Maybe the kid would like their own electric toothbrush. Lots of kids love having ownership of their own tools and using them like adults. Having their own teeth-brushing kit could be a way to emulate Mom and Dad before going to bed. A pleasant atmosphere, without fear or anxiety or compulsion, opens the door to games and other fun options to add to or modify the teeth-brushing experience. My wife and I make a big deal about how good our breath smells after we brush. We huff in each other's faces after brushing and then playact being overwhelmed by the amazing smell. Our kids love to join in and dazzle us with their minty fresh breath.

This might sound like a cheap trick to get my kids to do my bidding, so I'll give another example.

Little kids often draw on the wall. Few rules seem more reasonable to a parent than "Thou shalt not draw on the walls." I'll admit, the first few times it happened in my home, it was quite hard for me to suppress the urge to tell my daughter that there was no drawing on the walls. How could I possibly discover a win–win here?

My first step was to consider: What appeals to a kid about drawing on a wall in the first place? Easy: It's a large, broad surface that's always available and doesn't shift under your marker when you press on it. The next step was to figure out how I could re-create these features of the wall to my daughter's satisfaction *and* make it easy for us to clean up. We decided to get some large drawing paper and set our daughter up on the dining room table. I taped down the edges so it wouldn't move and made sure she had all the supplies she needed. We placed her on top of the table so she didn't need to struggle with the chairs.

She would still draw on the walls sometimes, so we upped our game. We bought markers that wash off easily, and also bought some extra wall paint and cheap brushes so that we could achieve 100 percent cleanup if we really needed to. Eventually we got her an easel so she always had a broad surface to draw on.

With a solution this good in our back pocket, on the rare occasions when she drew on the walls, we could afford to take some time setting up an alternative drawing surface and congratulating her on her work before suggesting switching surfaces. We still asked her not to draw on the walls, and our creative alternative that she enjoyed helped generate an understanding of *why* to stop using the wall infinitely more than simply telling her to follow the rule would.

In the end, it was a beautiful win–win. We made a system where all the kids have easy access to the art supplies, and it is easy for us to clean up. And our kids almost never draw on the walls.

Pushback against these examples comes in the form of what-ifs. What if the kid says she doesn't want to draw on the paper and keeps drawing on the wall? What if she draws on the wall when we're not looking? What if she draws on the couch?

The key is to keep trying to figure out what it is they like about drawing on the wall, and then providing that in a tidier way. If the kid refuses and keeps drawing on the wall, I know that my alternative isn't as fun and that I need to try something else.

What tends to happen instead is that a less fun alternative is forced on the kid, like drawing in a sketchbook. It's no surprise that a toddler, having had a taste of using that big, broad wall, is not satisfied with the sketchbook and tries to go back to the wall.

If you can figure out what the essential elements of fun are in a certain situation, and then re-create and even amplify those elements in a related situation that better suits *your* needs, then the what-ifs melt away.

When we pull off win–wins, like making teeth brushing fun or re-creating the wall-drawing experience in a way that is easy to clean up, we not only avoid the Foul Four, but we create practically the opposite. Instead of becoming a gatekeeper and adversary, the parent becomes an agent of fun. We become someone our kids want to have around because, instead of blocking their interests, we aid them in fostering their interests and make their world more open and exciting.

And notice that, while win–wins are not rules, they are also not neglect. In fact, they are very child-focused and often a good bit of work, at least early on. And they are not a mixture of rules and permissiveness. They are something altogether different.

For the rest of this chapter, I will present the basic process of *taking children seriously* in the context of a few more examples.

STEP ONE: UNDERSTAND THE PROBLEM

The first thing I do when I encounter a problem with my kid is pause and try to better understand the problem itself, or the problem situation. This is the basis of discovery, yet it is very common to rush past this step and start looking for solutions. When the kid is drawing on the wall, the temptation is to yank the marker out of her hand, but that's a bad solution because it's not accounting for the totality of the problem—in this case, that she is enjoying herself doing something you'd rather she not do. Tearing the marker away from her might solve *your* half of the problem, but because this solution doesn't take the child's half of the problem into account, the purported solution causes a host of avoidable problems that we discussed in Chapter Four.

In order to figure out *why* my daughter is drawing on the wall—that is, in order to better understand the problem she's solving for herself—I will sit down and draw alongside her. This opens her up to showing me what she's doing and why she likes it. Often, just immersing myself in the problem is enough for win–win solutions to percolate up spontaneously. Ideas come to mind, like taping a large sheet of paper on the wall and directing her toward that.

I also reflect on whether the problem is really even a problem at all. My kids will often spill stuff on the floor while they're involved in some project. Rather than interrupt their flow, I'll glance and see if the floor is dirty already. If it is, I'll just let them spill and then vacuum when they're finished.

My oldest son likes to use my shampoo when he's taking a bath. He'll spend forever playing with the sudsy water and endlessly pouring water in and out of my empty shampoo bottle. Rather than tell him to stop, I realized that my shampoo isn't any different than a set of extremely fun bath toys *from his perspective*, and he gets very clean as a result. Now I just buy shampoo in smaller bottles and keep several extras under the sink, and I don't buy bath toys.

I also spend time focusing on the problem situation even when I know I almost certainly won't solve it in the moment, like when a toddler has a tantrum. I'll still focus on what is going on and try to get ideas about what has driven this kid to scream inconsolably so that I can prevent it in the future. There's no shame in failing to come up with a solution in the moment, so long as you continue to think of how you might find one for next time—there is almost always a next time.

Exploring the problem situation of your child produces several dividends:

1. It helps you bond with your kid. There's nothing like sharing the moment, especially when it's a moment that breaks the conventional rules and adds novelty to otherwise staid adult life.
2. It helps you understand what makes your kid tick, what it is about the world that interests and delights them. This is a superpower, because it enables you to convert almost any boring or unappealing experience into fun.
3. It switches your role from being on the outside as a nag or a stern enforcer into a curious and explorative insider, partner, and guide.

STEP TWO: GUESS SOLUTIONS

Trying to guess win–wins is much more fun than enforcing rules. It requires creativity and inventiveness, and when you succeed, the payoff is not only satisfying, but it can be used again and again. A win–win solution can permanently eliminate a problem from your and your child's lives.

The trouble is that there is no recipe for this. I can't tell you how to think up a candidate solution. A nice thing about rules is that they are easy to describe and implement. But finding win–win solutions requires creative discovery, for which there can never be a set path. If there were a reliable way for any parent to get any kid to eat vegetables without producing the Foul Four, every parent would already know about it and there would be nothing to discover.

Fortunately, our minds are inherently creative. Coming up with new ideas is more about giving the mind the time and space to think and explore than it is about doing any particular thing. This is why step one, understanding the problem, is so important and cannot be rushed—the more you learn about the whole problem situation, the more ideas simply pop into your head.

One thing I've learned to do is adopt an overtly playful and even goofy mindset. This worked amazingly with my son when he was a baby. He *hated* having his diaper changed. I would pin him down with one hand as he writhed and screamed, while I furiously changed him with the other. It felt awful to restrain him like that, but I justified it on the grounds that I simply couldn't let him sit in filth. I eventually realized that I was using my mind to rationalize the severe treatment I was administering to him, rather than using my mind to figure out a solution that both he and I were happy with. *Is there really no way to make changing a diaper fun?*

To have any hope in finding a win–win, I needed to lighten up. So, the next time I went to change his diaper, I just tried playing with him. I found myself hunched over him, singing a goofy song and rocking back and forth while he giggled. Somehow, I managed to get him changed, all while rocking and laughing. It was messy at first, but the more I tried it, the more I got the hang of it. After a few trials, I made a simple discovery—he didn't mind having his diaper changed if he was standing! Thereafter, I'd just walk him over to a low table, put a toy on it, and change him standing up. No screaming, no crying, no struggling to get away as his stern-faced father held him down "for his own good."

I would never have found the standing-up solution if I remained convinced that there was no fun way to change a diaper, because I wouldn't have been open to exploring the space of possible win–win solutions. The trouble with rules is that they close off the search for better solutions and instead settle for a certain amount of suffering. Aren't our kids worth that search?

To emphasize, a win–win solution won't always arise from nowhere. In this case, the interim solution of rocking with the baby while changing a dirty diaper wasn't great. It required a fair bit of strength and dexterity, not to mention courage. But rocking was a stepping stone to other solutions, with the eventual discovery of a win–win so simple that it could be easily replicated by others. Whenever anyone else took care of him, like my parents, I'd show them how to change him, and they too could help him be comfortable and clean without the screaming session.

STEP THREE: TEST GUESSES, CYCLE THROUGH IDEAS, EXPECT FAILURE

The vast majority of ideas don't work, and this can make the whole approach feel idealistic and futile. A crucial element of Taking Children Seriously is to understand this ahead of time, to expect any given idea to fail, and to never try to force it to work. That's the problem with rules—they are an attempt to force a solution to work while ignoring the collateral damage. Seeking win–win solutions, on the other hand, is an attempt to improve on bad solutions, reduce collateral damage to zero, and replace it with fun. Doing this requires dropping bad ideas so you can focus on thinking up better ones. It requires resisting the temptation to try to justify a bad solution, and instead actively looking for better ones.

Recently, my three-year-old had a nasty impetigo rash and needed antibiotics. Of course, she was reluctant to swallow the medicine, and my explanation that she needed it wasn't getting through. As the loving parent of a sick and vulnerable little girl, it is incredibly tempting to say that this medicine is non-negotiable, and then force her to swallow it. But I fought that temptation and allowed alternative ideas to come up.

Later, she wanted an ice pop, and I suggested she dip the ice pop in the tiny cup that dispensed the medicine. She shook her head no. Then I considered mixing it in her food but worried that she might catch on that I was tricking her. I tried showing her the rash and talking about how uncomfortable it was and how she'd surely like to make it go away. I tried telling her about what medicine is. None of it worked.

Rather than torture myself about finding a solution, I busied myself with other stuff I needed to do so that my mind had more time to come up with ideas. She didn't need to swallow the medicine urgently. It just so happened that one of our babies also had an infection and I needed to give him a dose as well, so I began to prep the tiny baby syringe we use to squirt the medicine into his mouth. My three-year-old loves to help with everything, and she asked me if she could give the medicine to her baby brother. I saw my opening, and while my three-year-old fumbled with the syringe, I used baby talk to tell the baby why the medicine was important. My three-year-old copied me, as she so often does, and the two of us sat there speaking baby talk, telling him over and over why it was so important to drink his medicine and how it would help him feel better. When we were done, I simply placed the three-year-old's medicine in a cup next to her and said in the same cheerful tone, "Here you go, honey." She downed it in one gulp and proudly showed me the empty cup.

This example might seem implausible. What am I going to do when my daughter needs medicine and we don't have a baby to playact with? The answer is that I'll have to think of something else, although now I have some ideas to work with, some stepping stones. Maybe I'll use a doll next time, and we can pretend that my daughter is the doctor. Or maybe she'll give me some fake medicine and then I'll give her the real medicine in return. Or maybe we'll pretend my daughter is the teacher explaining to a class why medicine is important.

There are several important points in this example. The first is that failure is part of discovery. The path to a nearly flawless solution like the one I found almost always includes several bad ideas along the way. And when it becomes clear that an idea is a flop, just drop it and move on. And then, when you do find a solution, you can keep this in your back pocket for next time.

The second point is that the number of possible win–win solutions is infinite. This curious fact becomes evident when you consider turning the situation into a game, because games can themselves be infinitely modified.

The abundance of possible solutions is *the* bulwark against all types of cynicism. How could you ever know for sure that you're not on the cusp of discovering a brilliant solution? The fact that there are infinite solutions out there inspires me to remain optimistic that I can find one.

The third point is that win–win solutions are extraordinarily specific to the problem situation at hand. Therefore, the better you understand the problem situation facing both you and your child, the more precisely you can tailor the solution. This is a powerful feature of Taking Children Seriously, because it gets you in tune with them, helps you get to know them, and helps you and your child be open to each other. It's hard to think of anything more worthwhile.

CONCLUSION

Seeking win–win solutions avoids the pitfalls of neglect on the one hand and rule enforcement on the other. I have outlined a four-step process here, but I don't mean to suggest that there is anything like an algorithm for success. Finding win–win solutions is genuine discovery, and there is no roadmap to discovery. There is instead a list of suggestions, such as not being afraid of failure or remembering that a win–win is always possible.

Everyone is able to think up new options. The deciding factor is whether you allow yourself the freedom to relax and explore, or whether you fixate on how unacceptable it is, or dangerous it is, or unhealthy it is, if you don't get your way. You might tighten up from a need to show strength and resolve as a rule enforcer, or fear that if you aren't sufficiently tough, your kid will walk all over you. If your search for an alternative solution to the problem at hand is really just a quick peek, and if you find nothing, then you are going to drop the hammer and enforce the rule, then you're really not allowing your creativity to work. Once you adopt an expansive mindset, solutions start appearing, often simple and obvious ones.

Taking Children Seriously is just a commitment to remain open to a brilliant idea as long as you can.

Chapter Six

COUNTERARGUMENTS

QUESTIONING RULE ENFORCEMENT GENERATES A predictable set of objections. In this chapter, I use the most common ones to develop the underlying theory of Taking Children Seriously.

WHAT IF YOUR KID RUNS INTO THE STREET?

This is without a doubt the most common objection, and it gets stated as an almost ineluctable proof that *some* rules are necessary. Now, before going further, the answer is no, I would not let my kid run out in front of a car. There is nothing wrong with grabbing someone and forcing them away from danger. We'd do the same for an adult in our lives if they had *inadvertently* put themselves in harm's way. To be sure, we'd only do this if it was clear and unambiguous, like if they were unknowingly backing toward a cliff edge. We wouldn't impose our will if they knowingly wanted to do something dangerous, like riding a motorcycle or smoking cigarettes.

If a toddler goes running in front of a car and you scoop her up just in time, she may not recognize that you just saved her life, and yes, she might generate some resentment that you spoiled some of her fun. But rather than give her a stern talking-to about the dangers of roads and the need to follow the rule, you could instead try to understand what attracts her to playing in the street and try to provide that in a safer location, like the backyard. Maybe she likes the wide open space of the street, or the feel of the pavement under her feet, or the simple fact that people chase her when she runs toward the street. Fortunately, it's relatively easy to make a backyard more fun than the street. We put up a fence so that the kids won't be able to suddenly run out into the street. This also keeps items like balls in the yard, and keeps out unwanted threats, like dogs. (The fence may seem like a limit, but if the kids want to leave, we make the gates easy to open. This is an example of a voluntary constraint.)

This describes the situation for a street outside of a home, but what about the sidewalk of a busy thoroughfare? What if your kids are doing what kids often do, which is get excited and run around unpredictably? Are you really going to stand there and watch? As always, what I would do depends on the specific situation and which of the infinite number of solutions I might find. I might put a kid on my shoulders to get a more fun bird's-eye view of what's happening—if he's willing, of course. I might point out to my kid how big and fast the cars are, and that I can hold his hand to keep him safe. If instead he wants to horse around on the sidewalk, I might pretend we are special agents on a mission to get to our destination undetected, and that we need to stay close to the buildings and away from the street in order to stay hidden.

Sometimes my wife and I are not in the mood for the contrivance of a game, so we do "intense mode" instead. We might find ourselves in a busy parking lot, and we'll tell the kids that we're shifting into intense mode, which means we're all adopting an efficient, no-nonsense, focused attitude to watch for cars and get quickly out of the parking lot. I like intense mode because it's very honest and explicit about what's going on. Often I'll narrate loudly, "I'm watching that car. Its backup lights are on, and I'm not sure if the driver can see us." Again, this might be a bit involved at first, but after doing it a few times, it becomes an extremely quick, safe, and fun way to get a bunch of kids where they need to go. As I'll describe over and over, Taking Children Seriously often requires a sizable investment in the beginning but produces large savings of time and effort later on.

THESE GAMES ARE JUST MANIPULATIVE TRICKS TO FORCE KIDS TO DO WHAT YOU WANT

No, for two reasons. The first is that they can opt out. If one of my kids doesn't want to do intense mode, I don't make her do it. I try to figure out why she's objecting so that I can improve intense mode and mold it more to her liking. Or, I'll simply do something else for the time being, like carry her. I definitely wouldn't want to taint intense mode by guilting or chiding her into conforming, because if she ends up resenting it, then I lose it as a tool.

A requirement for fun is the freedom to opt out. Rejecting an activity provides feedback that helps me further refine it and make it more fun. Refining *rules*, on the other hand, means crafting them so that they can more precisely squash a child's opportunity to express herself, learn about the world, and have fun.

The second reason it's not manipulation is because the games are genuinely enjoyable. My kids are truly entertained by them and play along willingly. They also know that what they're doing is a game, so I'm not tricking or deceiving them as a real manipulator would do.

Rules, on the other hand, are a contrivance that we tell kids are real. "There is no running in the street" is presented as if it's an objective fact about the world, as simply and unavoidably true as the fact that day follows night. In reality, you *can* run into the street, and the rule is just made up. Enforced rules are manipulative falsehoods about the world.

One could say the game is deceptive because fun can be used to hide an ulterior motive, such as getting them to go to a place they don't want to go to. For instance, I might trick them into going to the doctor's by making a fun game that requires the kids to get into the car, through the parking lot, and inside the office where they are surprised to find they are getting a shot. That would indeed be deceptive if I hid from them the fact that the game is a lead-up to visiting the doctor, but doing so would be disastrous. The kids would notice the betrayal and they'd become suspicious of my games in the future. Any good thing can be used for bad ends.

THIS WOULDN'T WORK FOR ME. I'M NOT A CREATIVE PERSON.

You'd be surprised. Once you get in the habit of allowing yourself a minute to think, new ideas begin to pop up out of nowhere. One time, we were vacationing with friends, and they were getting ready to leave for the long car ride home. Their son wanted to watch a show on his tablet, but his battery was low. His parents told him he needed to make a choice—he could watch the show now, but that would kill the battery and he wouldn't have his tablet available during the car ride. His parents clearly wanted him to have the tablet for the ride so that he wouldn't complain to them that he was bored. But they also wanted to support his autonomy by letting him make the choice.

My wife, an expert win–win discoverer, simply got him an extension cord so he could charge his tablet and watch at the same time. Everyone was suddenly relieved as the parents realized their kid could watch now *and* later. In retrospect, the extension cord seems so obvious, but at the time, we were all fixated on getting their kid to make the choice we wanted him to make.

I DON'T HAVE TIME TO LOOK FOR WIN–WINS

Yes, forcing the issue gets results fast, and dreaming up alternative solutions can take lots of time and effort. However, finding a win–win tends to *save* you time in the long run. Once a kid is enjoying scampering safely through a parking lot, you might find they are less resistant to leaving the house. Once they are enjoying brushing their teeth before bed, you have more time in the evenings.

Ironically, a life of rules *creates* a sense of urgency. For rule enforcement to maintain credibility, it must be swift and reliable. If the parent pauses before enforcing the rule, then this gives the kid an indication that perhaps this rule is optional after all, especially if it is resisted with sufficient resolve. And if a parent bends on a rule even once, it is hard to regain that sense of unquestioned inevitability. In a bid to appear rational and gentle, modern parents may tolerate a question or two about a rule, but these questions are really an opportunity for the parent to explain the otherwise inflexible rule. Effective rules must be enforced quickly, before suspicion and resistance can grow. Hence rules create urgency and baseline anxiety.

Even more importantly, if you are never an adversary, if you never give kids a reason to be defensive, then you save an incredible amount of time and effort by not battling with them. When a judgmental gatekeeper asks you to do something, there's a tendency to get your guard up. Often, when a person is in a defensive posture, the knee-jerk response to any request is "No." This baseline resistance takes lots of time to overcome. The old-school way of breaking this resistance was to be severe, threatening a beating if the parent detects "talking back" or "lip." But if you are fun to be around, then kids are more open to your suggestions and honoring your wishes. They are more trusting of your explanations about why you'd prefer they do this or not do that.

Also, the wins build on themselves. Once you find a game that works in one situation, you can use that game in others, varying it to suit the context. As you find out what your kids' interests are, you can utilize them to solve problems. Our son got obsessed with octopi, so we got him cheap octopus figurines that entertained him for hours on long car rides. Rather than waste time and effort managing a grouchy toddler in the car, we found a solution that fostered his interest *and* gave us a happy passenger.

And finally, once you get good at exploring the space of possibilities, you find that solutions come to mind more quickly. Having faith that solutions are findable, and scoring some surprising wins, can turn you into a confident problem solver.

One way to start out with Taking Children Seriously is to just build in sixty seconds of brainstorming about possible win–wins before issuing any command. Even if you're in a rush, you almost always have sixty seconds to spare.

A common conflict is trying to get the kids in the car for an appointment when they are reluctant to stop what they're doing. When I'm in a rush, it's agonizing to sit there and think up ideas. A trick I use to buy myself time to think is to get myself completely ready first. I get my shoes on, gather up all the stuff I'm bringing and place it at the door, and finish all other necessary preparations until I am ready to walk out the door. This usually takes a few minutes, and in that time I can always think of one or two ideas to try out. Most of the time, my kids notice I'm prepping to leave and, because they regard me as trustworthy and fun, they come to me while I'm getting ready. This does half the work, because now they've voluntarily paused what they were doing and are open to my suggestions of an alternative.

The truth is, with most conflicts, you have far more time than sixty seconds. Being in a rush for an appointment is our fault for not getting ready to leave five minutes earlier. With the teeth-brushing example, you don't have to figure out a win–win solution for brushing teeth at that moment or even that night. There are zero consequences for not brushing for one night, or even several nights, or even several weeks if we're honest. And if we're talking about baby teeth that will fall out some day, is there even a reason to brush these at all? This is another happy consequence of taking the time to think of win–wins: Sometimes, you realize that you can simply drop your demand altogether.

Forcing the issue gets quick results, but these results are a mixed bag. It gets some of what you want, but it also gets you some of the Foul Four. And, if it produces a perpetually sullen and defensive kid, it might cost significantly more time in the long run. On the other hand, time invested in finding win–wins *also gets you what you want*, as well as other happy dividends (fun, trust, openness to suggestions and explanations), and none of the Foul Four.

WHAT HAPPENS WHEN I CAN'T
FIND A WIN–WIN?

I often run out of time while thinking up novel solutions. When I do, I sometimes force my preference on my kids—reluctantly. On several occasions, I have picked up a screaming toddler and placed them in a car seat, pinning them down while I strap them in. However, when I do it, I don't add insult to injury and blame the toddler. Instead, I apologize and look for ways to make it less objectionable by offering a toy or a snack.

Taking children seriously doesn't mean that failure never happens. But failing to find a win–win is a different type of failure than the failures of enforcing a rule for several reasons. First, trying for a win–win that doesn't work is at least productive, because you learn something not to do that makes success more likely later on. I'll often reflect on what didn't work and come up with several ideas for next time. Second, the failure is a one-off event, which means it's easier to recover from. Kids are less inclined to think of you as an adversary when you make it clear that it was a mistake that you'll try to fix, rather than a pattern that they should get used to. Some adults rationalize these patterns as "life in the real world," but the real world doesn't force adults under the boot of authorities. Third, if you can credibly blame the failure on yourself, this spares the child from internalizing it.

"I forced you into the car because I couldn't figure out a better way to do it." Not because the child was in some way inattentive or selfish or otherwise not performing up to expectations. Yet it is common to hear parents justify their coerciveness as a necessary response to the kid's supposed degeneracy.

If you are late leaving for work in the morning, is it really the kid's fault for not hustling into the car? Was it a surprise that you had work today? Did you really not know that the three-year-old needs some coaching and support when transitioning from being in the house to the car? Is that three-year-old "being difficult," or is the parent being unreasonable? Should the object of your frustration really be the three-year-old?

It's intuitive to implement rules out of fear of failure, and an orderly household where the kids are all following along with rules and expectations may seem like a success. But even when rules are supposedly working well, they guarantee that all current failures are locked in and can never be resolved. Enforced rules ensure that stasis is the law of the household, that progress toward genuine solutions is blocked off. If you're really worried about failure, rules are the problem, not the solution.

SURELY YOU'D INTERVENE FORCEFULLY IF YOUR KID WANTED TO DRINK ALCOHOL OR DO DRUGS?

Small children don't have an interest in drugs and alcohol, so thankfully it's not an issue until their teenage years. And even then, drugs and alcohol don't just appear in the course of a normal day. Plus, there are plenty of warning signs that something is wrong before a kid actually accesses and uses drugs. After all, the kid is pursuing destructive behavior *for a reason.* With Taking Children Seriously, a parent addresses the child's drift toward self-destructive behavior by striving to better understand the kid's problem and think up solutions. In other words, the broad strokes of the solution are the same for any other problem that the child may face. The details and severity may differ, but the basic problem-solving process I described in Chapter Five remains the same.

Some parents will respond, "Don't be ridiculous. In a situation as dire as this, imposing rules is worth not having a dead kid." But self-destruction happens in households with rules, too. There is simply no way to guarantee that such a dire issue won't arise. What Taking Children Seriously offers that traditional parenting philosophies do not is that the parent will serve as a trusted resource and guide in the child's life. The hope is that, when dark ideas and influences arise in the child's life, they have no qualms about approaching their parents for advice.

And this all-purpose problem-solving approach applies to much more than substances. It includes media content, relationships with friends and romantic partners, and physical risk-taking. A warning from a knowledgeable and trusted person who knows you and cares about you, delivered in a nonjudgmental way, is a very effective lifeline. It should be cultivated and preserved at all costs.

But this carefully cultivated sense of trust is fragile. Rules enforced in one area—say, food—can taint the efficacy of this lifeline in other areas, like drugs or sex. All the more reason to strive, not just to reduce rules, but to eliminate them altogether.

The inverse—children falling down a dark path and hiding it from their parents—is so common that it's a trope in television and movies. So much for the success of enforcing rules to ward off self-destructive behavior in kids.

WHAT ABOUT VERY BASIC RULES, LIKE "NO HITTING"?

When someone hits, they are imposing their will on the other person. They are denying the other person the option to solve the problem or opt out. The victim of aggression can only flee or fight back, and in a household, fleeing is not an option. Since the whole purpose of avoiding rules is to avoid the Foul Four, then a parent can't allow kids to hit, kick, or otherwise assault others. Aggression is the antithesis of taking the other person seriously. Preventing kids from hitting is preventing them from being tyrants over others.

Nonetheless, a rule like "no hitting" is a mistake. Why? My kids and I spend a lot of time wrestling and horsing around, which involves a lot of contact that often crosses the line from fun to unfun and sometimes devolves into aggression. If I told my toddlers "no hitting," that would *prevent* them from understanding where the line is between play and aggression. This is admittedly a very fine distinction that shifts dramatically based on the context. In an angry confrontation with a stranger, even the slightest contact can be assault, whereas a rowdy group of friends can have a lot of fun wailing on each other. A "no hitting" rule destroys the ability of kids to discover these nuances.

I've seen lots of playful jousting among little kids get shut down because the supervising adult imposes a zero-tolerance policy for physical contact. Not only does such a rule stop the fun, it also confuses what is otherwise a very subtle process of discovery. Even worse, it diverts the focus toward the adult. If the boundary of appropriate contact is set by the adult, then kids have reason to appeal to them any time they feel aggrieved. This sets the stage for a particularly destructive trope—the cry-bully who uses the slightest contact as justification for the adult to punish the other kid. The children's focus should instead remain on the problem inherent to the interaction itself, with the kids discovering and communicating to each other where their boundaries lie.

While (unwanted) aggression must be stopped, it still matters how this is done. The aggressor cannot be allowed to hurt the victim, but that doesn't mean the aggressor should be punished. Kids hit out of ignorance and frustration at not knowing another way to solve their problem. Like all other problems, this one is solvable by better understanding the problem situation and thinking up alternatives that resolve the conflict. If two kids are fighting over a toy, you can get a second toy or find something better for them to play with. Punishment and discipline in this context makes the parent an adversary and confuses the issue by shifting the focus from the conflict itself to what the parent thinks about hitting.

I will develop this further in the chapter on sibling conflict.

CONCLUSION

In general, there are two rebuttals to arguments that favor rules. The first is simply a reminder that rules always cause collateral damage—the Foul Four—and that they can always backfire, producing the very harms they're intended to avoid. The second part is to explain that any given problem can be solved by creativity, given enough time. This part of the argument is more difficult to make, because how people solve a particular problem depends on the nature of the problem situation. Any particular problem between people is rich with idiosyncrasies that are critical to the eventual discovery of a way forward. Problem situations and their solutions are like a river—no one steps in the exact same one twice. This is why it is not always obvious how any given problem can be solved without recourse to rules.

I have given some examples to show how finding win–wins between parent and child can be done in practice. Doubtless, readers will continue to think up "what if" scenarios. I am confident that if I could spend some time in first-person contact with the situation, I could address every "what if." You can too.

Chapter Seven

MORE EXAMPLES

ONE CRITIQUE OF TAKING CHILDREN SERIOUSLY IS THAT it is heavy on philosophy but short on practical applications. This chapter is a collection of basic applications with brief commentary, roughly organized around the course of a day.

MORNING

My kids wake up whenever they wake up—we don't use alarm clocks. My oldest chose to go to kindergarten, and if she wakes up late, we drive her to school on our way to work.

We rarely urge our kids to hurry—this is one of the biggest impositions on kids, a telltale message that their interests are frivolous. If they're late, they'll hurry if they value the thing they're late for. If they don't hurry, it indicates that they don't care, and so neither do we. It's a nice way of filtering out activities that they don't value, so their time can be spent on things they do.

When parents shuttle their kids around to activities that the kids aren't passionate about, they are eating up time that could be spent in search of something they *are* passionate about. A state of boredom and inactivity has the virtue of leaving a kid open to discovering a passion, while a state of apathetic activity closes kids off to new passions.

When they wake up, the first thing my kids want is their tablet and warm milk. I drink coffee and scroll on my phone.

BREAKFAST

We generally skip breakfast. Sometimes a kid will want cereal. Sometimes a bar of chocolate. My oldest likes "chocolate sandwiches," which is Nutella on bread. It's easier and tastier than peanut butter and jelly and nearly identical in terms of nutrition.

Instead of sit-down meals as a family, my kids snack. We have snacks available at all times, visible and within easy reach. Favorites are chocolate bars, Oreo cookies, chips, and dried cereal. Caffeine Free Diet Coke is another favorite. We carry a bag of these nonperishables on trips, so there's never a need to stop what's going on in order to eat.

LEAVING

When we leave the house, I never announce to the room something like, "Okay, we're leaving; it's time to get your shoes on!" Instead, I sidle up to my kid and, after waiting a few seconds, ask if they want to get in the car. If they brush me off, then I'll continue working on all the other things I need to do before leaving. I will make sure that I'm 100 percent ready to go before really focusing on them. I always hated being badgered to get ready, only to have to wait at the door for the badgerer.

While I'm getting ready, my kids often notice that I'm leaving and become interested in what I'm doing. This usually happens when I'm tying my shoes at the door. Sometimes I'll open our sliding door earlier so that the sound indicates to them that I'm leaving. They often wander over and ask me where I'm going, my answer to which often interests them enough that they get dressed and come with me.

This is how I get them from A to B in general--I go there myself and see if my kids voluntarily drop what they're doing and come toward me. This is worlds better than me going to them and commanding them to stop what they're doing and go somewhere else. It's hard to give a small child a reason in words for why they should stop what they're doing, but my "mere" actions can be persuasive.

We take care to avoid being in a rush. For predictable departures, like dropping the kid off on the way to work, we build in a few extra minutes to help make the transition relaxed. Often, adults are in a rush of their own making, and they blame their kid for dawdling.

Nonetheless, mistakes happen, and I often find myself hurrying the kids to the car. My younger daughter likes to linger on the threshold, pointing out all the outside things that delight her. "Look, a squirrel!" "There's water on the deck!" "What are these?" "Is that a bug in the stones?" This isn't dawdling, it's discovery--a toddler doesn't know when the appropriate time for inquiry is. I try to engage with her excitement, but if I really have to go, I'll just pick her up and carry her off. It breaks my heart to squash her curiosity.

If the kids aren't excited enough to get themselves in the car on their own, I often drop their tablet in their lap and scoop them up. If they object, I take no for an answer and try out some problem-solving. My default is to create a game, like offering to race to the car. For my oldest, I'll use explanations about why I think she'll enjoy doing what we're about to do. I'll often solicit her to help get her siblings excited to go. Unless there is real urgency, I never force a kid into the car and instead cancel the trip or try to find someone to stay behind.

Sometimes, my explanations fall flat. When that happens, I give up. I don't want my kids to develop negative associations with my explaining things to them. A verbal explanation is a superpower, and being unable to explain things to kids is almost the entire problem of being a parent to young children. Parenting could be summarized as the process of dealing with dependents who aren't understanding what they're told. When explanations do work, it's a miracle. But when they don't, talking devolves into a kind of punishment, driving a kid to simply agree in order to get the talking to stop, or to prepare defenses against the next conversation. I'm keen to avoid this, so when I notice words aren't working, I abandon them immediately.

Leaving fun places is difficult when the kids want to stay and the parents have had enough. I don't resolve this by declaring that "We're leaving." I also don't soften the blow of departing by setting a timer. Instead, I try to solve the problem by creating some fun. Or I create an alternative destination before arriving home, like going for ice cream or getting a treat at the gas station. Getting a treat lends itself to going home better than simply leaving the park. In general, I try to set up another fun thing to do that makes going home more seamless and enjoyable than simply declaring that time's up, the party's over.

I've explained to my oldest that figuring out when to leave the park is one of the difficulties of going there in the first place. On days we do go, I ask her what she thinks about agreeing to leave at a certain time. This works in about half of the cases, but sometimes she changes her mind once she gets there and wants to stay longer. I don't hold her to the prior agreements.

Adults can be held to contracts, but kids often don't understand and deserve some leeway.

A bigger challenge occurs when siblings are divided—one wants to leave while others want to stay. We don't invoke a vote and hand authority to the majority. Doing so would forestall problem-solving—there's always a win–win, and a vote followed by force is not a win–win. It's also important to understand *why* a kid doesn't want to go along with the plan. Votes ignore the reasons of the minority, and sometimes these reasons are better than the majority's. Voting can deprive all parties of the best options. There are times when votes are appropriate, such as when everyone agrees ahead of time to settle something that way, or when there's no time to figure out alternatives. But routinely appealing to a vote is routinely embracing a tyranny of the majority, and the majority often recognize who they are (my two girls, in my case) and gang up on the minority (my son).

When they disagree on when to leave, I make an effort to entertain the kid who wants to go home, again harnessing the superpower of being able to create fun. I try to fix what's bothering him—maybe he's cold; maybe he's hungry. Failing that, I try to facilitate some bargaining among the siblings. I also appeal to going for ice cream, the treat that almost always supersedes other options.

THE CAR

The car is an important problem situation to master. Many kids aren't "good travelers," which really means that the problem of being tied to a seat for unknown periods of time has not been solved for them. Since the car is essential for mobility in suburbs like ours, it is crucial to figure out how to make it a welcoming environment. Even short trips can become a problem for small children, since they can't distinguish between short and long trips.

To make the car more welcoming, I focus on entertainment, food, and drink. Tablets with headphones are the easiest answer for entertainment, but we also include toys and anything comforting. We also invested in a remote start so the kids don't have to contend with a cold car in the winter months.

Every time we leave the house for more than a few minutes, I bring nonperishable snacks. Since we keep a supply of "junk food" readily available for the kids, it's easy to sweep a few containers of cookies or chocolate bars into a bag as we're walking out the door. Kids report hunger at the darndest times, and even short trips can become an ordeal if a two-year-old starts screaming for food and is not satisfied to hear that we'll be home in five minutes.

SCHOOL?

We have full-time caregivers for our kids during the day while my wife and I work. Our oldest attended preschool and kindergarten but has opted out of first grade. In general, we follow the unschooling model, where learning is guided by the kids' interests. Rather than instructing kids in reading and math in an academic environment, we wait until they encounter a reason to use reading and math in their regular lives. The idea is that instruction sticks when it is delivered *after* the kid sees a reason for it and is interested to learn more. Our caregivers stock their day with plenty of encounters—trips, projects, digital apps, and anything that is fun. The kids plan and cook meals, manage plants and animals, and try their hand at entrepreneurship. All of these things offer a purpose for reading, writing, and math, as well as science, art, and civics. But more importantly, they don't give my kids a reason to hate these subjects. Any subject that is important enough to be taught in school can be made relevant in a project at home. These subjects become tools they use to get what they want, rather than obstacles to overcome in order to be set free when they go to college at the end of childhood.

My kids socialize with each other, their neighborhood friends, and their cousins. They visit centers for self-directed learning as well as public spaces like the library and playgrounds. We enroll them in activities they're interested in, like dance and sports.

OUTSIDE CLOTHES

When going outside, I don't make them wear any special clothes. If it's cold, I make their coats, hats, and mittens available and say something suggestive like, "Boy, it's cold out. I'm getting my mittens to make sure my hands don't freeze." If they decline to do the same, I don't belabor the point by asking them if they're sure or warning them that they'll regret it. The point is for them to figure out the trade-off between comfort and the restrictions of extra clothing, not to project onto them the expectations and anxieties of their parents. Mittens make it harder to use your fingers, and kids may prefer to have cold but usable fingers. If we're going to be outside for extended periods, I stuff extra mittens and hats in my coat pockets. When their hands get cold, I don't admonish them for not listening to me; I just give them their mittens.

THE PLAYGROUND

When our kids are on the playground, we try to leave them be, although other parents sometimes draw us in by policing how the kids are playing. Often a parent is declaring that the slide can only be used one way, or that kids need to take turns on this or that apparatus. I try to stay out of it, but if I get the impression that my kid might get bossed around by an adult, I linger. I tolerate a little bossing to give my kid a chance to figure out how to deal with such situations, but as soon as I get a sense that it's not improving, I step in. My stock phrase is, "She's okay," which often does the trick by conveying that we're not adhering to the policy and that everything is actually fine just as it is. If it's not working, we go to a different part of the playground and I make that area fun.

A trickier situation is when another kid—usually an older, bigger kid—comes over and declares that my kid needs to share or take turns. Again, I try to stay out of it and intercede only when my kid is not making progress. "She's okay" works with other kids, too. If they protest about sharing rules, I just ignore these declarations rather than try to explain myself.

INTERRUPTING

We let our kids interrupt us almost constantly. It is extraordinarily annoying. My wife and I talk with each other on the phone a lot because it's so hard to have an extended conversation at home. Our reasoning is that talking is among the most important skills kids develop, and we don't want our kids to hold back. As novice talkers, it is difficult for them to understand what their audience considers important, and so they blurt out whatever comes to mind. I know many adults who lack the restraint required to let other people talk and mistakenly think that whatever interests them must be equally interesting to everyone else.

Reprimanding a kid not to interrupt doesn't help them discern what is worth speaking about and what isn't—it just makes them reluctant to share what's on their mind.

When my wife and I need to speak with a third party, our strategy is to tell our kids directly—but in a pleasant tone—that we need to talk to so-and-so for a minute and that we'll talk to them later. With small children, we do this sparingly because we want them to feel encouraged to talk to us. Household speaking rules reflect a tacit assumption that kids are second-class, that not only their interests but their opportunities to speak are always trumped by adult airtime.

We also honor this in reverse. Our kids will often object to our explanations of things and tell us to stop talking about it. We almost always respect these requests and change the subject—if the message isn't landing, persisting is probably just adding frustration to the confusion.

HELPING OUT

We don't make our kids clean up after themselves, mainly because they don't understand why. They don't value cleanliness, so if we forced them to clean up, this would just seem like an arbitrary requirement, a pain point for doing messy stuff like art or building forts out of couch cushions.

We want our kids to enjoy painting for the sake of painting, and to see us as coconspirators in fun endeavors, not as nags who make painting a little less fun. If the price of this is that we clean up after them, so be it. Besides, kids are bad at cleaning up, and we probably spend the same amount of time cleaning up after their cleanup effort. Plus, there are ways to make cleaning up easier: I prefer devoting my efforts toward obtaining washable paints, large containers for easy pickup, and disposable materials.

Making kids clean up is often more work and takes longer than cleaning up yourself *and* risks the Foul Four. I can clean up an entire room in less than five minutes—hardly an overwhelming burden. I'm confident that, eventually, my kids will learn the value of cleaning up after themselves as a courtesy to others, if they don't develop an appreciation for cleanliness themselves. This is also why we don't make them do chores. We don't want to ruin their understanding of the value of participating in the care of a home by instilling in them a resentment and avoidance of these things.

In fact, cleanliness is not always a virtue. Serious artists and craftspeople have workshops that remain in disarray so that they can immediately pick up where they left off when they return. Constantly cleaning up takes time and saps some creative energy and knowledge embedded in the placement of tools and materials. Ideally, kids would have their own workspace that can remain disorderly, allowing their passions to burn.

At home, my wife and I have an agreement—any time our kids want to help, we stop what we're doing and figure out a way to get them involved. One evening, I was staining our fence and working quickly to finish before it got dark. My daughter wanted to help, but I knew I couldn't finish in time while also preventing her from making a colossal mess. But I took sixty seconds to think and realized that there was a part of the job she could contribute to—brushing the dirt off the fence posts. She loved that I was in a rush and helped me finish quickly. We had a ball.

I resolved that, no matter what, I would never turn my kids away if they wanted to "help out around the house." Even if it slows me down or creates a lot more work overall, involving them voluntarily is an opportunity for them to learn to value things like cleaning and repairing. Today, our six-year-old routinely volunteers to help clean up, simply because she enjoys making everyone happy with a tidy living room. And our three-year-old helps prep almost every meal. The five-year-old isn't into it, but I suspect his time will come. It's just a matter of him discovering "work" that he enjoys.

DISCIPLINE AND PUNISHMENT

We never do either. The closest I'll get is with our six-year-old when I tell her that aggravating her younger siblings makes work for me. Rather than discipline, this is more of an appeal to her to be more understanding and forgiving. One peculiarity I've noticed is how difficult it is to convey to a child the idea of being understanding, of giving others some slack or the benefit of the doubt. It's interesting that such a crucial concept is so difficult to put into words that a child can understand. At first, I thought this was a deficiency of language, but now I think it shows how the norms of civility are really quite subtle. Discipline and punishment run roughshod over these subtleties and make it that much more difficult for children to discover them.

Discipline and punishment, and coercion in general, never get kids to do anything. Instead, they raise the costs of doing something else. There are many ways to raise the costs of pursuing alternatives, from simple beatings or threats of beatings, to shaming, withholding possessions or denying privileges, or sequestering them to listen to lectures. If a person does something because alternatives are made too unpleasant, they tend to do the bare minimum in order to obtain relief. They do it to satisfy the disciplinarian, not themselves. The resulting learning is thin, based on a performance, and only loosely connected with other knowledge.

Discipline and punishment show us what Taking Children Seriously is not. Rather than raising costs to get a certain behavior, Taking Children Seriously *lowers* costs to get *understanding*. Specifically, costs are lowered in order to open up freedom for curiosity to search for and discover knowledge, and knowledge that works forms an understanding. Parents are cost reducers and freedom promoters.

BODILY OWNERSHIP

We make it clear to our kids that they own their bodies. If their faces are snotty and dirty, we ask their permission to wipe them clean. If they don't want to wash their hair or take a bath, we take no for an answer. It took a long time to gain my son's confidence to let us wash his hair—the big issue was soap in the eyes, and now he holds a washcloth over his eyes until the shampoo is rinsed out. It took many months to discover this system, and his hair smelled pretty bad, but we decided nice-smelling hair was not worth the trust that would be sacrificed by smearing shampoo on his head and ignoring his screams.

This policy got put to the test recently when our daughter had a nasty splinter. It was big and began to look infected. She started getting frantic about the pain, and my wife and I got worried about the need to treat it with antibiotics. Nonetheless, she refused to let us even come near her with the tweezers. We started thinking that maybe we had to force the issue when we had a timely visit from a friend. Her daughter had similarly refused splinter removal, and they had used a topical anesthetic cream. By applying it under a bandage, the splinter had worked itself out on its own. We gave it a try, along with some antibiotic ointment, and the problem was solved painlessly.

VISITING AND TRAVELING

When we go somewhere that is adult-focused, like visiting family, we create ways for the kids to opt out of adult activities such as sitting around and talking. Our primary strategy is bringing their tablets and making sure they have movies and games downloaded for periods with nothing to do, such as long car rides. There are of course many ways to do this—the important thing is that we don't expect our kids to conform to adult standards of being with others. Yes, it's important to be able to handle boredom, but only if you understand why--for instance, if you understand that it's a sign of respect to sit and listen to an older person tell stories that you're not interested in. But if a kid doesn't understand that, then being bored in front of Grandpa just makes the kid resentful of visiting Grandpa, which is the opposite of respect.

For the same reason, we never make our kids greet extended family. Forced greetings and the like disrupt the growth of bonds that create intimacy with others. Similarly, forced thank-yous for gifts and forced apologies for mishaps like spilled food or broken tchotchkes disrupt the discovery of the subtleties of expressing gratitude and regret by contaminating the process with shame, fear, and embarrassment. When a loved one gives my kid a gift, I say thank you. I talk about why it's so thoughtful and what I'd imagine my kid will do with it. If my kid breaks something or makes a mess, I do my best to make amends, but I don't involve my kid in cleaning up. It's hard enough to be in an unfamiliar place with unfamiliar people, and mistakes are inevitable. Plus, my kids didn't even choose to be there, and they don't have the option of simply leaving when they feel uncomfortable. All of this is plenty of reason for me to unburden them from figuring out the intricacies of being sociable.

One strategy for meeting up with people that you want your kids to form a relationship with is to meet somewhere fun, like a playground or science museum, so that the kid is not confronted immediately with a strange home, possibly with strange smells and otherwise not structured with kids in mind. Another strategy is to prepare the visit with a new toy that is revealed at the family member's home that the kid can play with. Including a big, fun activity like going to a water park can be too taxing for some grandparents. A simpler alternative is a trip to a big-box retailer like Walmart to pick out a few toys that can be brought back to Grandma's home. This provides a trip, which is often fun in itself. You can add in a stop for lunch, and then the fun of running around the store and mulling over the toys. Instead of blanching at the cost, consider how much money you're saving by not going to a water park.

At home, we often go to the grocery store or the convenience store just for fun. These places are incredibly stimulating and exciting, with lots of options to explore, especially when we're not on a shopping trip and not in a rush. Kids get exposed to the idea of prices, money, and saving up to buy stuff they want. We let them put pretty much anything they want in the cart but only actually pay for a few items at checkout. One way to let them pick what they want while maintaining an eye on cost is to go to a Goodwill Store. We don't police their interactions with others or hector them about making a mess—we just put things away when they leave them on the floor. We often sneak in a pizza meal at the food court and a little bit of adult shopping to boot, an incredible win–win.

FEELING TORN

One summer morning, our three-year-old suddenly declared she didn't want to go to camp. We were blindsided. She had been having a lovely time, the counselors adored her, and every time we picked her up she was engrossed with the friends and activities. Why did she suddenly protest? When we asked her, she couldn't give us a coherent answer. What to do?

This happens quite often in various circumstances. For example, we recently got in the habit of taking our kids to the gym. There's a supervised area for kids to play while we work out, and our kids were having a blast. Then, the four-year-old declared he didn't want to go anymore. The temptation to force him to go was strong. After all, we had watched him having fun before and we knew he would very likely enjoy it again. We tried to persuade him, but when he didn't budge, we violated our principles and forced him to return to the gym more than once. Every time we did so, his initial cries of protest eventually shifted into squeals of glee when he started playing with the toys. We patted ourselves on the back, weakly telling ourselves that applying force had been the right thing to do. But it wasn't.

When kids don't want to do what we know they will enjoy, they are experiencing the same thing adults experience when we put off doing something we know *we* will enjoy. Part of us wants to exercise, wants that endorphin rush and the satisfying, fresh feeling that comes after exercising. But part of us doesn't want the discomfort, the sweating, and the hassle. To resolve this, we often treat ourselves the way we treat our kids— we force the issue. We bully ourselves into "making the right choice." Instead, the solution is to inquire about the dilemma, to better understand the problem, and to try to resolve our internal conflict.

This is hard enough to do as an adult, let alone as a kid. Paying attention to why they might be resisting and addressing those concerns is an obvious strategy. A technique I use is to make video recordings of how much fun they're having at a given activity. When the time for this activity comes up again, I'll play the video as a reminder of the fun they were having, so they can keep that in mind as they mull over their inner conflict.

DINNER

As I mentioned in Chapter One, we don't have family dinner time. Instead, in the evenings after work, my wife and I make food for each other and invite our kids to have some. They usually decline, and we make them the food that they like. We don't force them to all come to the table at the same time, and instead set food up for them wherever they are in the house. Most of the time they'll sit at a flat surface because tables make it easier to watch a tablet and eat at the same time. We only set the table for dinner when we have guests, but the kids are still free to eat wherever they want. Our oldest likes to join in and participate in the conversation, and the three-year-old likes to emulate our oldest. But our five-year-old doesn't like to sit at the table and talk, so we don't make him.

From this, it may not seem like family mealtime is very important to us, but the truth is the opposite. Relaxing and talking freely with family over a meal is among the most important things, and we want our kids to learn why it's so valuable. Therefore, we don't want to contaminate their understanding of this by forcing them to be with us, forcing them to eat what we're eating, and forcing them to sit and be bored in our presence.

BEDTIME

As I described in Chapter Two, our kids don't have a set bedtime. They approach sleep the same way as the adults in our home— if they're tired, they crash early, and if they've got something interesting going on, they stay awake for it. Otherwise, all the kids tend to head upstairs when the day feels over. Our oldest does the usual bedtime prep like washing and brushing teeth on her own because she likes it; the other two are hit-or-miss, but almost always brush if we suggest it and help them. As for getting the kids to sleep, there's a mix of reading books and watching tablets, and usually one or two of them want some form of company, but there's no real process.

A REVEALING ANALOGY

When my oldest daughter was five, I took her along on a cross-country trip. We had fun navigating the airport, riding the escalators, sampling the airplane food, and exploring the hotel. Much of the drudgery and stress of travel was transformed as I experienced it vicariously through my daughter, and in the process I rediscovered my role as parent.

Here she was in a strange land, with all sorts of things and people she'd never dealt with before. Having journeyed well outside of her comfort zone, she had plenty of reason to be afraid, to feel vulnerable and disoriented. I found myself being more forgiving and patient than usual of my daughter's minor slights. When she tripped in the airport hallway, I was quick to comfort her because I wanted to reassure her that, even though things were strange and different, her father was there, not only to protect her but to help her engage with these new things in a way that was fun *and* safe.

It struck me that life on the road is really the same as life back home, just amplified. Everything is new to a child, and their default state is vulnerability and ignorance mixed with curiosity. They need to learn about and engage with elements of life that adults take for granted but are new for them, and they should be totally forgiven any mistakes or misunderstandings.

My role as parent is as guide and protector, not manager. To support my daughter's discovery and eventual mastery of the world, it's at least as important that I avoid making her feel nervous, afraid, and bad about herself as it is to teach her.

A LITMUS TEST TO AVOID FOOLING YOURSELF

Improvement requires error correction, and error correction requires error *detection*. Many strategies for softening or eliminating rules merely obscure their coercive nature, allowing them to persist under the radar. Fortunately, there is a simple test to check if a rule-reducing strategy still contains coercion or not, and that is to switch the roles from you and your child to you and your partner or spouse.

Maybe you're considering positive reinforcement to get your kid to brush their teeth. What would your spouse think if you showered them with praise when they did something you want? Might they grow suspicious of your accolades and begin to feel patronized? Maybe you're considering rewarding your kid with a treat or a toy for doing what you want. What would your spouse think of these kinds of rewards? Might they resent being treated like a pet, as if all they cared about were the treats and were too thick-skulled to understand why you want them to do what you want?

Maybe you want to force an issue that is just obviously in their best interests. What would your spouse think if you physically forced them to do what you "just knew" they needed to do? Might they object, saying something like, "If it's so important, why can't you explain its importance to my own satisfaction?" You might reference your greater knowledge and understanding of the situation, but then again, your spouse could reasonably ask, "If you're so smart, why can't you think of a way to persuade me? And if you can't persuade me, why can't you think of some other way of achieving your goal that doesn't require forcing me?"

Imagine your kid has the same eye for being manipulated that your spouse has: If your spouse were in your kid's shoes, would he or she find your behavior or words patronizing? Would he or she challenge you with the above questions, and could you answer them to your spouse's satisfaction? When trying to integrate Taking Children Seriously, these questions are a quick test to check whether or not you're smuggling in some coercion.

CONCLUSION

This chapter offers a picture of what life is like in our home and some sample solutions we've arrived at for typical problems. It's not a how-to guide for the right way to raise kids. The examples focus on small children because my kids are small, and also small children are particularly difficult to reason with. If you can make it work with them, it only gets easier as their store of knowledge and skills deepens. I can persuade (not manipulate) my six-year-old rather easily in most regards, and she is generally on board with my suggestions. As she continues to grow, I anticipate having a partner in the home who is largely aligned with my preferences for basic behavior and can help convey these to her younger siblings.

Chapter Eight

SIBLINGS

SIBLING CONFLICT MIGHT BE THE MOST DIFFICULT aspect of Taking Children Seriously. Conflict is hard enough to reason through when at least one party is adept at solving problems. When neither is, it often leads to chaos, suffering, and failure to resolve the conflict.

However, the temptation for an admittedly knowledgeable parent to get involved and help resolve the dispute between two siblings is a trap. A conflict between two siblings is *about the siblings*, not the parents. So, when parents step in, there is no way to ensure that the kids won't shift their focus away from their shared problem situation and toward the parent. Why is Dad yelling at me? Why is Dad siding with her? Why is he making *me* say sorry? Notice how similar this dynamic is to one of the unintended consequences of rules-based parenting—with rules, the child learns how to conform to them, rather than about the wider world. With parental intervention into sibling conflict, the children are prevented from learning how to solve interpersonal disputes and instead learn that their parents will arbitrarily intervene in their lives.

(Readers may balk at the use of the word arbitrary here—the reasons a parent invokes for breaking up a fight is anything but arbitrary. However, to the child, it will *seem* arbitrary because children don't understand the reason that fighting isn't the right thing to do. That's why they're fighting—they are ignorant of better alternatives, of better applications of emotions.)

As before, reasons are always paramount. Harmonious behavior is desirable only if it happens for the right reasons—mutual enjoyment and appreciation—rather than fear of punishment.

BOUNDARIES

Most sibling conflict is really just ignorance or confusion about boundaries. As I described in Chapter Four, boundaries are the limits a person sets on what they are willing to offer others in terms of time, personal space, and resources.

Living with others is a constant test of boundaries. Navigating them is tricky, even for adults who already know what boundaries are and how they work. Groups of adults can rarely sustain living together in close quarters simply because their preferences rarely align. One likes loud music, another likes smelly food, and so on. The groups that do sustain communal living tend to only do so by suppressing members' divergent preferences, usually by appealing to some binding authority such as that found in a monastery or cult.

For kids, it's even worse—at least monks and cultists can opt out! In a typical familial household, kids' preferences are made to cohere with those of the adults through the binding authority and explicit tenets of the parents. To maintain "peace" and "stability" in the home, kids are indoctrinated into uncritically accepting things that radically violate their innate sensibilities. School is similar in this regard, as young students are often made to believe that freedom is bad, boredom is good, and drudgery and anguish are virtues. And in school, like in many other areas, a child's boundaries are determined by someone else.

Living in harmony with others requires communicating and negotiating boundaries. To do this, we must know what our boundaries are and respect ourselves enough to assert them. And this requires understanding and developing our own preferences. I discussed developing preferences and tastes in the chapters on food and sleep as they pertained to one's personal development. Here, we see that authentic and deeply held preferences are also essential for social relationships because they are fundamental to one's boundaries. Parents may worry about the health consequences of letting their kids eat and sleep how they like, but they rarely factor in the impact of under-nurtured preferences on the health of their relationships.

If I am passionate about music, and my housemates are passionate about quiet, then the solution is not for me to simply not enjoy music in the house or to inflict noise on them. Ideally, I would create an alternative that works for everyone, like a soundproof space to listen, or invest in good quality headphones, or some such other solution. If not, we're probably not going to get along.

Kids need time and practice in order to learn boundaries, and for the most part adults tend to give kids lots of leeway as they learn the ropes. But kids don't know how to give other kids leeway. If one kid invades another's personal space or so much as touches their toy, they might fly off the handle. Kids often deliberately transgress boundaries just to provoke a reaction. For young siblings, these transgressions and the resulting chaos hang over every minute spent together, putting parents on near-constant alert and anxiety. What to do?

The temptation to apply rules is almost overpowering. Chaos is degrading for everyone, and this is one of the best arguments against totally permissive parenting. For the sake of everyone, it is understandable that a parent must "lay down the law," establishing that there's no hitting, no yelling, and that everyone must be generally quiet and peaceful.

Rules laid down in this way might achieve the *appearance* of peace—though of course there's no guarantee and they can always backfire—but rules don't help kids learn boundaries. Rules teach them the opposite—that *other people* set the terms for how one should behave, and that communicating and negotiating personal preferences have nothing to do with it. In any case, they might just learn to dupe these authorities and transgress a sibling's boundaries anyway. Worst of all, the Foul Four that inevitably come with enforcing boundaries might harden into a lifetime of bitterness and coldness toward their siblings and parents. Solving interpersonal disputes *builds* relationships, and top-down rules prevent this mutual discovery and social development from happening.

So how do you help kids learn to develop and communicate boundaries while also preventing chaos? The essential question of this chapter is just a version of the essential question for every other topic in this book: How do we support learning, understanding, and discovery—and their engines: curiosity, freedom, and autonomy—while also avoiding a household full of chaos and strife?

STAYING OUT OF IT

As much as possible, avoid getting involved in conflict. I avoid even being in the same room, so that the kids don't suspect they are being surveilled. This helps them focus on the nature of the conflict itself (the problem situation) and see what kind of response their actions receive. Each kid can give an honest signal about how they're feeling, both verbal and nonverbal, and the sibling can observe the totality of it and send an honest signal back. Even if it doesn't lead to a resolution, it does lead to learning and progress. The next time conflict looms, they will both have some idea of what the other's preferences are, and what the costs are of violating those preferences.

Letting kids sort things out can quickly devolve into screaming, and it can seem like their relationship is irreparably harmed. But while small children don't yet understand the nuances of conflict resolution, they haven't learned how to hold a grudge, either. They may yell and declare their undying hatred of their sibling, only to return to playing together minutes later as if nothing happened.

I don't leave my kids to scream and fight for any extended period of time. As soon as it becomes clear that they're not making any progress—screaming, crying, and hints of violence—I jump in and intervene. But I try to give them enough time for their conflict to either resolve or devolve. Often, kids' play will oscillate in and out of conflict as they bump up against each other's boundaries. I would hate to forestall their opportunities for practice.

On many occasions, my kids will have a big blowout, with name-calling, crying, and storming off, and I will question myself for not stepping in before things devolved. It hurts to see them fight, and I really want them to get along and enjoy each other's company. But, on at least half of these occasions, one of them eventually asks why the other got upset, or even volunteers an apology. When this happens, I thank my stars that I had the fortitude to not get involved, because if I had, it would have ruined this reconciliation.

Why bother reconciling on your own when the adult does it for you? There's little reason to notice when your sibling is getting upset if you've never been responsible for dealing with the chaos that follows. You don't need to look for cues that they're open to reconciling if the adult announces them for you. And if "sorry" is the magic word that the parent declares will end conflict by fiat, then when a kid says it, there's no reason for him to pay attention to his sibling's body language to see if his apology actually worked.

Reconciliation is nuanced. Even adults struggle to put these intricacies into words, so it's not surprising that it's nearly impossible for small children to do it. Successful reconciliation requires careful attention, and this comes from *wanting* to get it right. People who don't want to resolve their conflicts don't resolve them. But if an adult intervenes in a child's conflict, there's no reason for the child to focus on what their sibling is doing, or even to notice that resolving conflicts is something the child can do themself. Instead, the child's attention shifts to the adult, who becomes the mediator. For example, if a child doesn't like how their sibling is using a toy, they're more likely to appeal to the adult than address it directly with their sibling. This can lead to constant pestering for the adult to settle disputes—and worse, manipulation, where one sibling tries to turn the adult against the other.

Another issue with intervening in sibling conflict is that the adult almost never knows what's actually going on. Typically, the adult just wants the yelling to stop and isn't particularly interested in the cause. But even a well-meaning intervention invariably makes incorrect assumptions about who did what, and kids often unwittingly affirm these assumptions in an effort to appear agreeable or "in the right." Or, kids might just say what they think the adult wants to hear in order to get the adult out of their business. Or worse, a kid might take the opportunity to manipulate the adult into blaming and punishing the other sibling.

When I do intervene, I try to ignore whatever they are fighting about, because I don't want my involvement to confuse whatever the issue is that they are fighting about. I also don't want them to redirect the anger that they have toward each other onto me. Instead, I look for a quick way to neutralize the conflict without making it about me.

If they're fighting over a toy, I grab an extra from somewhere and wordlessly present it to them. I don't include a lecture about getting along or being nice.

If I don't see a quick solution, then I often join in their play. I try to create enough fun that the previous conflict becomes irrelevant and harmony reestablishes itself. Through the course of the entire episode, the kids get some practice dealing with conflict, but I stop it before it comes to blows *and* without inserting myself as a bungling and authoritative party.

As my kids get older, I sometimes complain about the consequences of them fighting, without addressing the nature of the fight itself. I'll say something like, "It's really annoying when you guys yell; can you play without being so disruptive?" Or, "I really don't like it when you two fight; can you try to keep it fun instead?" This is similar to how I would treat a fight between my father and my brother. I wouldn't insert myself into the details of the dispute, because I wouldn't presume to know the issue better than they do. Indeed, it would be strange for me to stand up and declare that my brother is right and my father should back off or go to his room, as if I have special knowledge of the situation that they both lack. But I would complain if, for instance, their bickering was disrupting dinner. This is another example of using the litmus test described in Chapter Seven.

As I've said before, staying out of conflicts and only intervening when they start to get out of hand does require a lot of effort. However, in the long run, it results in *less* work, as my kids more quickly learn to read each other's signals and get along. Kids who can entertain each other without conflict require very little work.

THERE'S NO "NO HITTING"

One of the most compelling rules to make is "No hitting." Adults are duty bound to prevent kids from getting seriously hurt, and from hurting each other, so an adult cannot tolerate hitting. Therefore, what's wrong with stating explicitly that hitting is never allowed? Well...a lot.

My kids cherish visits from their cousins. Being older and bigger than my kids, they can handle full-strength punches and kicks from my kids. The result is fun-filled melee. I can't imagine extinguishing the squeals of delight just to enforce a "no hitting" rule. Not only would this kill the fun, it would also interrupt the familial bonding at work. One special thing about family is having more intimate relationships where you can do things, like wrestling or tickling, that would be inappropriate with others.

Rough-and-tumble play amounts to a literal crash course in boundaries, including how they shift based on the context. The boundaries between family are different than those between friends. Boundaries also shift based on intent. Invariably, when my kids are roughhousing, one of them will take something personally and start to use punches and kicks to truly hurt someone. This change in intent becomes obvious by their flushed face and absence of smiles or laughter. As the intention shifts, so do the boundaries. A punch from a three-year-old means something very different when she is smiling and giggling as she delivers it than when she is yelling and crying.

Like all rules, a "no hitting" rule is too obtuse to accommodate these subtleties, and so it blocks the ability to learn them. All of the context and intention get reduced to "hitting," and the *reason* for hitting gets dismissed. This doesn't teach gentleness or kindness—in fact, it achieves the opposite. Kids who aren't free to send and receive signals develop a blunted sense of what's really going on in the other person's head, of appropriateness, and a reduced ability to read other people.

BREAKING UP FIGHTS

Letting kids figure out their boundaries while keeping them safe is challenging. We cannot let a larger child beat on their little sibling, but how do we prevent such a thing without imposing rules?

The crucial point is that kids always fight because of ignorance. If they knew how to appropriately get angry (as civilized adults do), or how to get what they wanted with words rather than fists, they'd do that, if only because verbal persuasion preserves relationships while fists degrade them. Our hope is for kids to learn these things quickly so that they can enjoy the company of their siblings and build mutually supportive relationships.

Unfortunately, small children are rarely open to simple explanations about the best way to prosecute one's anger.

My approach is to listen from the periphery for signs that play is deteriorating into a fight. When I hear the telltale signs,

I take a glance. If I see that violence is imminent, I insert my body between the two parties, blocking the blows. When I do this, I make an effort not to appear judgmental. The best way I've found to do that is to simply stay silent. My presence alone makes it obvious that I don't want them to hit, but if I start *verbalizing* that, my kids, in their heightened state of awareness of any slight, might interpret it as a reprimand.

I never admonish the aggressor. Instead, I console both the aggrieved and the aggressor. This can be very difficult, because neither of them tends to be interested in sharing my sympathy with the other. The aggrieved feels more deserving of consolation, but the aggressor is often the one who is suffering the most (psychologically). But since they don't fully understand why they are upset, they almost certainly won't understand a reprimand, either. Their oppositional state primes them to conclude that their parent is against them as well, which is the last thing I want them to think.

Later, when tempers have calmed, I sometimes bring up the conflict to see if they are open to reasoning about it. I again take care not to present this as a punitive talking-to. If I get the sense the kid doesn't want to talk about it, I let it go. Usually, I don't lead the conversation toward a point or a lesson, I just let them practice putting words to their emotions and the facts of the events. If I see an opportunity where a morsel of knowledge might be welcomed, I usually phrase it as an example of what I do in similar situations. "When I get mad at someone, like Grandpa, if I hit him, that just makes the problem worse." With our six-year-old, I'm often more direct. "Since your brother is younger than you, he doesn't know that taking your toy is annoying. Someday he'll learn, just like you did."

Reprimands and punishments for hitting and even injuring a sibling might seem necessary, particularly to instill a sense of justice and deterrence against future fights. Don't kids need to learn justice? Yes, but the question is: *How* is the best way to learn it? Reprimands and punishments in the moment are unlikely to be understood in the way that you intend. But they will always produce the Foul Four. They damage trust, make kids feel bad about themselves, confuse the issue by making the behavior about avoiding punishment rather than about doing what's right, and reinforce a system of authority as the means to achieve harmony.

When I first started breaking up fights without issuing punishments or reprimands, I felt guilty, like I was turning a blind eye to something bad. This was especially so in front of family or close friends. "You're going to let him get away with that?" But now it feels very comfortable, and I'm reassured by how little my kids fight. I can't imagine disciplining our kids. Disputes are no more common in our household than other places I've been, and they are settled rather quickly. One thing I find particularly reassuring is that my wife and I are not adding to the general level of strife in our home.

PREVENTION

The simplest way to prevent conflict is abundance. If a toy is desirable, we get several. Instead of putting limits on prized foods, we get extra. We replace scarcity with abundance as much as we can (and within reason).

A fun, absorbing toy can turn into a problem if it becomes the source of squabbling. The temptation is to take it away, or threaten to do so, in order to motivate kids to behave with it. But this gatekeeping redirects their ire from each other onto the parent. Worse, it replaces the kids' momentary fight with an even larger and longer-lasting cycle of discontent, as not only have the kids not truly resolved their conflict, but now they have reason to view the parent as a source of unfairness and frustration.

Buying toys in duplicate can get expensive, but engaging toys are quite valuable, for everyone. They open up time for parents to do other things, and happy kids are easier to take care of. I think of buying duplicates as investing in harmony and supporting family relationships, not as spoiling my kids.

Worries about spoiling children play into the Greedy Child Fallacy, which erroneously tells us that it's bad to get what we want. "Spoiling" is only a problem if it distorts a child's understanding of the world, including what it takes to get what they want. If there's no reason to prevent a child from playing with a fun toy, then there's no reason to prevent a second child from the same.

Another tool for preventing conflict is deploying the fun-creation superpower. Fun renders many conflicts irrelevant and dries up conflict's wellspring: boredom. Playing games with kids takes time and effort, but it teaches them games that they can play on their own. More importantly, it shows them that creating fun is always an option and empowers them to conjure up fun on their own.

The idea that boredom incentivizes kids to learn how to entertain themselves is often just a rationale to ignore kids. Children need some ideas to get started, and if adults play childhood games with them, this seeds them with games that they can later play on their own.

OWNERSHIP

Our kids own their stuff and get to decide what happens with it—we never tell them they have to share, or that they have to take turns with it. One reason is because that is confusing.

I know that sharing my car with a stranger in need may be a kind and thoughtful thing to do, but if I was forced to do this, I'd still have questions. Why me, why my *car*, why this particular other person, and if an authority has the power to decide what I do with my car, in what sense is the car mine? Do I really own anything?

Forced sharing would make me careful about my car. I'd want to conceal it. I would bitterly complain if I had to share my car more than others shared their stuff with me. If this forced sharing was a pervasive norm in the world, then to get stuff, I'd look at my neighbors' possessions and then appeal to have them share those with me. If I wanted to target an enemy, I'd identify his most beloved possession and accuse him of not sharing it, just to spite him. Sharing is forced on kids to teach them to be kind and generous, but instead it inculcates them into a mindset of possessiveness, envy, enmity, and suspicion.

My kids readily share with each other voluntarily because they're not worried about scarcity. If my daughter wants to share her ice cream but then runs out, I get her more. On the contrary, many parents will declare that the supply of ice cream is fixed—you only get one, and when it's gone...it's gone, because that's life, you can't always get what you want. But that's *not* life—you can, in fact, almost always get more ice cream. Life is figuring out the trade-offs between getting more ice cream and doing other stuff with your time and money. Imposing an artificially fixed supply of ice cream fosters anxiety and territorialism among siblings rather than generosity and restraint.

Since the system of private property works well for adults, we should give that system to kids. We shouldn't force them to use some other, inferior system until they're old enough to join the adult world where property is privately owned. That would be like teaching them incorrect physics until they're old enough to learn the physics that adults use.

When my kids receive a gift, that becomes 100 percent their property. If they treat it poorly, say by using it for unfit purposes or smashing it in anger, we don't stop them. When they throw their tablets in frustration, we don't chide them for misusing their stuff (that would just add to their frustrations). Instead, we invest in quality cases. Once again, my purchase doesn't "spoil" my child but is an investment in their personal and social development.

Yes, there are pitfalls to personal ownership, but there are issues with every system. At least the pitfalls of private ownership apply to the adult world as well, so learning to deal with them as a child pays off.

When a friend drops off a gift for the kids without specifying who it is for, my wife and I try to clarify ownership before it gets presented. If everyone wants it, I go and buy a few more. If that fails, we try some creative problem-solving, such as agreeing to joint ownership, or making a trade so that one kid takes ownership of the new item in exchange for an old toy.

One trick is to have a hidden stash of cheap gifts for each of the kids. If a new gift arrives for one of them, I unveil the others so that everyone has something.

If we buy one large, expensive item for all of our kids to use, then we consider it to be the property of us, the parents, and we parents set our own admittedly arbitrary rules about how it gets used. Since these rules apply to what we own, then what we're really doing is setting boundaries that our kids can opt out of if they want. Even in this kind of situation, it's best to find win–win solutions unconstrained by rules, but property rights at least give all members of the family a first pass at understanding how to coordinate with one another given a limited resource, such as a television.

You may be wondering: But if parents own all of the property of the home, why shouldn't they also establish rules for everything, from bedtime (after all, they bought the beds) to rules around food (they bought the groceries, the cookware, and the stove)? Answer: Because children are dependent on their parents to live; they cannot opt out of living in their parents' home. They have no choice but to sleep, eat, bathe, and spend leisure time in the home. Under such circumstances, establishing unbreakable rules in all the ways we've discussed so far would indeed be coercive and therefore run into the Foul Four.

Another pitfall is using someone else's property, like a swing at someone else's house. If nobody is playing on the swing, and my daughter decides to hop on, this often draws the attention of my son who then demands a turn. I don't make her stop and give him a turn because it just doesn't seem right to me—he wasn't interested until she started using it. I remember as a kid how annoying it was to discover something fun, only to lose access to it when it drew the attention of others who were less inquisitive. Instead, I might try to entertain him while she swings. If this fails and he's so insistent on swinging that he starts pestering her, I prevent him from aggressing her until she's done.

Fortunately, young children's attention spans are usually brief enough that prolonged standoffs like this are rare. Older children have had more time to learn politeness, especially if they've had the freedom to practice authentic interactions with others and have discovered the relationship-preserving benefits of being polite and courteous. My oldest will often acquiesce to her younger siblings because she understands this too.

In the end, creative problem-solving trumps ownership. The other day, my oldest was playing with her younger sister's doll.

When her sister grabbed onto one of its limbs, my oldest started yanking at it, shouting "I had it *first!*" I intervened, forcibly separating my oldest from the doll. She protested loudly about the need to share. While I was mid-sentence in reaffirming property rights, her younger sister realized that the doll had a twin and went and got it. Suddenly my words were irrelevant, and everyone was happy. One worry about a focus on property is that it reduces relationships down to transactions and fairness and turns a blind eye to problem-solving, like seeing if there is another doll that might represent a win–win.

In this particular dispute, as with all problems, the space of potential solutions is infinite. Maybe there's a game where both children can play with the doll, or there's another doll, or another toy can substitute, and so on. Ownership and property rights are not infallible rules, but they *are* the default to fall back on in the absence of problem-solving, the best known way to seamlessly and continuously coordinate who gets to use what.

EVERYONE GETS THEIR OWN SPACE

Adults rarely engage in physical conflict. I've discussed one of the reasons—they understand boundaries and how and why to control their emotions (really, knowledge of how to appropriately emote). But the other reason is that adults have a place they can withdraw to if they don't like how they're being treated. This ability to opt out of dealings with other people is crucial to individual peace of mind and also social harmony. Just knowing that you have an exit is reassuring, even if you don't exercise your ability to use it.

Kids, on the other hand, are typically denied this option. They are often in social situations outside the home, most notably school, where they must face the close company and interaction of people they may not like, who may even show them outright physical hostility. One of the arguments for school is that kids need to be exposed to the real world, but in the real adult world, we would never force someone into the presence of a physically hostile adversary. And our advice to a friend who is being physically threatened at work would be to sue or at least quit.

Within the home, kids are often stuck in close quarters with no option to exit. Conflict in this scenario is simply unavoidable.

Retreating to a private space is a kind of conflict relief valve, and it is particularly important for kids because they don't have the knowledge of how to signal and negotiate boundaries, and they don't have full command of their emotions. Locking kids who don't yet have the means to deal with others peacefully in a shared bedroom is a recipe for physical and emotional strife.

Each of our kids has a place where they can close the door and not have to interact with anyone. My two oldest kids use this frequently. They both have tempers, and when they fly into a rage, they'll often storm off. It is upsetting when this happens, and at first I was tempted to chase after them and try to address the issue. But I realized that they went to be alone because they *wanted* to be alone—and there's nothing wrong with seeking privacy.

When kids are fighting, we want them to stop and mull it over, but when emotions are strong, this is nearly impossible. Going to their room provides that break in the action, giving kids the ability to opt out of any conflict and go think about it, or do something else. For this to work, they need to be able to close off any unwanted intrusion.

When they do go to their rooms, I don't want them to think that I don't care about them, but I also don't want to intrude. My process is to give them a few minutes by themselves. Then

I tap on the door and ask if I can come in, while also taking no for an answer. If they let me in, I use open-ended questions like "How are you doing?" or "Do you want to talk about what happened?" Then I just act as a sounding board, essentially acknowledging that they're upset, offering insight only if it's asked for, erring on the side of serving as a passive listener.

There are plenty of other reasons for creating private spaces. If a kid wants to do something disruptive to others, like play a loud or rambunctious game, it's great to have their own room in which they can run wild. If the family is being rowdy in the living room—maybe we're playing a boisterous parlor game—and one of our kids doesn't like the noise, they can escape. And if we have guests that they don't particularly like or are not comfortable around, they can escape them as well.

An individual, private room doesn't have to be big to work as intended, but it does need to have a door or closable barrier, preferably with a lock that forestalls a pushing match with a sibling, but which a parent can open in an emergency. It may seem like an extravagance, but I detect a bit of the Greedy Child Fallacy at work here as well. For adults, privacy is considered essential, almost sacred, but for kids, asking for privacy is often considered asking too much. Who are they to want what we adults have?

CONCLUSION

In a way, kids are worse off when they are in conflict with other kids than when they are in conflict with adults. At least adults have experience in managing their response and accounting for the other person's preferences. It's like getting lost in the woods—it's better to do it with someone who has traveled the terrain before than with a fellow newbie.

Kid–kid conflicts have the added difficulty that it is very hard for an outsider to help. Involvement almost always confuses the issue and exacerbates it. Nonetheless, solutions are always possible, and guiding principles can help. It is possible to achieve harmony while respecting conflicting preferences and not imposing rules from on high. That's not to say harmony can be guaranteed—no method can do this. But it can be achieved for periods, and those periods can be nurtured and reinforced such that they stretch out for longer and longer durations. The goal is for kids to learn to effectively signal their boundaries and read the boundaries of others.

By and large, try to stay out of it, and when you occasionally get involved, do it nonjudgmentally. When outbursts happen, pay attention so you can anticipate and prevent the next outburst. Abundance, clear ownership, and privacy are your friends.

Chapter Nine

STEERING THE FAMILY FROM RULES-BASED TO RULES-FREE

SWITCHING TO A HOUSEHOLD WITHOUT RULES MAY seem unreasonably idealistic, irresponsible, even utopian. Karl Popper, whose philosophy this book derives from, showed that utopias are impossible. It was known long before Popper that utopias rarely work, but he showed why they *can't* work, even in the best of circumstances.

A utopia depends on a vision of a better world. However, during the long journey to bring about that world, it is unavoidable that the understanding of the vision will change and that the visionary will make mistakes along the way. This causes followers to lose faith, which in turn causes the visionary to react with authoritarian measures in order to keep everyone in lockstep.

Popper's solution to achieving progress while avoiding these pitfalls was to pursue small, reversible changes that can easily be undone if the change proves mistaken. To improve the education system, the utopian would describe the ideal alternative in great detail (cloaked in moralistic language to recruit supporters) and then tear down the existing system so that none of the evil vestiges persist on the way toward the newly formed vision. Instead, Popper recommends improving a system by identifying *specific*, piecemeal problems within the system and fixing only those problems. In the education system, an obvious problem might be poor-quality textbooks. Replacing them with new books is relatively easy to reverse—the old books could be stored in the basement. But an even more reversible change could be adjusting the curriculum so that it doesn't even use textbooks, thereby avoiding the risk of spending money on new books that don't improve learning.

How does this apply to transitioning a family from rules to no rules? To be sure, such a transition would be a huge change, and we shouldn't be utopian about it. If your kids are older and have been living with rules and expectations for years, and you suddenly declare that the household has gone rule-free, this would cause big problems. For one, many kids wouldn't know what to do with themselves and might find the sudden lack of structure unsettling. They might fall victim to the popular confusion that an absence of rules means a license for mayhem. They might binge on previously restricted pleasures to an alarming degree, such as staying up all night playing video games or eating nothing but sweets for weeks.

Scrapping the system of rules throws out some good stuff, such as a harmonious home and plans for how to provide food. Suddenly removing rules would certainly produce chaos, and this probably wouldn't be fun, even for the kids. The real question is: How do we change from rules to no rules incrementally, one small, reversible step at a time?

We can start with the low-hanging fruit—say, a rule that nobody likes (even the parents). My personal favorite rule to dispense with is teeth brushing. Maybe stop insisting that they brush their teeth and instead try to make teeth brushing fun. Explore the range of different toothbrushes, toothpastes, mouthwashes, and flosses, and try to make it clear why you brush your own teeth in a way that is not a lecture. Personally, I emphasize the smell, because that is immediately evident and nobody likes having smelly breath. As for reversing, you can simply reinstate the rule if the experiment is not working. And even if it comes to this, I bet the teeth-brushing experience is improved with better brushes and toothpastes.

Parents of small children may be understandably anxious or fearful about switching from rules-based parenting to the kind for which I've been advocating. The typical stance toward rules is that modifying them is forbidden, because if they are modifiable at the parent's whim, then their arbitrariness becomes evident, and kids might become more resistant or resentful of them. However, if rules are presented instead as the least bad option that parents can think of to deal with a given problem, then this opens the door to improving the rule. The goal is to improve the rule so much that it becomes irrelevant, eventually replaced by understanding, freedom, and fewer run-ins with the Foul Four.

FOOD RULES

Food is a great area to experiment with relaxing rules. How about the one about finishing your plate before you leave the table—do "two more bites of your broccoli" make any real difference? Will those two bites per day prevent a broken bone or a vitamin deficiency? And if you really think it will, can you fulfill that deficiency some other way, like maybe by offering the kid a daily gummy vitamin?

Another experiment is to pick one meal per week or day during which kids can eat anything they want. It's possible that they will surprise you by eating relatively normally, and maybe you expand the number of days with no eating restrictions.

You could see if they want to plan and prepare the meal. You could take them to the store to find the ingredients and do as much of the meal prep as possible. You might find a meal that they truly like and enjoy making that doesn't violate your worries about health. Now you've discovered a win–win in which they feed themselves pleasurably and healthily. It's even possible that you could find several such meals and unburden yourself from a significant chunk of food preparation. And if relaxing the food rules "backfires" and the kids gorge on junk food, they may learn from the experience and avoid doing so again the next time they have free reign over their meal.

This is the beauty of Popper's incrementalism. It sounds simplistic, but once you start poking around at small changes, like experimenting with freedom around food, a world of new ideas can open up. There are infinite ways to make improvements, especially with something as variegated as food. There are different ingredients and types of preparations, and even if a change doesn't work, it can spawn other ideas that *do* work. Eventually, you might find healthy, tasty meals that are fun to prepare that would have otherwise remained unknown because you didn't look. After a period of experimenting, the way the family eats could be wholly transformed for the better.

SLEEP RULES

What are some candidate incremental changes to sleep rules? Move bedtime a half hour later and see if anything terrible happens. Move wake-up time later by streamlining the kids' morning routine (prep their clothes and a fast breakfast the night before) so they have more time to sleep in. Pick one night per week during which kids have no bedtime at all. Try having no bedtime for a whole week and see how things go.

For small children, the urge to keep them on a schedule of naps, ostensibly to prevent toddlers from having tantrums, is a major source of control and management. Instead of scheduling around naps, try a week of letting the kid fall asleep on their own and see if the resulting moodiness is more disruptive than the time and effort needed to maintain the schedule.

School is a major source of rules, not just in the schooling itself, but also in the homework, the need to go to bed early and wake up early, and all of the scheduling that surrounds school. What are small changes that can be made to reduce the burden of school? Homework is particularly useless. Can parents help reduce the homework burden, perhaps by simply asking the teacher to assign less, or by helping your kid do it quickly? Sometimes the first or last period of the day is a free period—can the student sleep in and arrive late or leave early on those days? Community colleges offer classes to high school students, so maybe a kid could replace part of high school with these courses, exposing them to more cognitively challenging subject matter while also acquiring college credit. Some community colleges offer summer courses to kids as young as eleven. Perhaps a kid could take courses during the summer, and, if they are sufficiently committed, use this as a transition to homeschooling. Maybe a parent could meet with the teachers individually and inquire about independent study whereby the student engages in a self-directed curriculum that meets the class requirements but unburdens them from being in the classroom and doing homework.

In other words, a parent could help to reduce the burden of rules on their child *at* school and provide an off-ramp *from* school. Can you unburden them from the bus? Can you increase their options during free periods? Can you increase their options during class? Can they test out of classes? Can they eat outside; can they eat at a local restaurant; can you take your kid out to eat lunch? Can a local grandparent take them out for lunch?

CHORES

One set of rules that can be done away with suddenly, without incremental change, is chores. In the past, chores may have been a necessity because the family needed the child's labor around the house and in the fields. Even in those circumstances, there are voluntary ways to enlist the child's help and make this labor fun, but leaving that aside, in modern life, forcing children to do chores simply provokes the Foul Four with very little to show for it.

Kids are just not very productive, and making them do things around the house often requires more work than simply doing it yourself. Like adults, children are productive when they have a reason to be. If the reason for doing chores is because Mom and Dad force it, then they only have a reason to do the bare minimum.

It's thought that by forcing kids to do chores, they will value doing work, recognize they are part of the family unit, and learn the importance of everyone doing their part. As with so many rules, the reality is the opposite. Forcing chores gives kids a reason to resent work, resent the family, and resent doing their part. If these things are truly valuable, then it's important that kids genuinely learn the value of maintaining the house, mowing the lawn, and taking care of younger siblings. Chores confuse these things (as all rules do) and make them seem like burdens that are only done because Mom and Dad say so.

I would rescind all chores immediately. That's not to say I wouldn't welcome help around the house from my kids—I'd simply start to *ask* them if they'd like to help and accept "no" as an answer. If my kids aren't already absorbed in something, I routinely ask them if they want to help set the table or clean up the house. Since they're young, I almost always do it with them and think of ways to make it more fun. My six-year-old now takes the lead on things like setting the table, and if I ask her to clean the living room, she usually jumps at it. And, since her younger sister likes to emulate her, I'm often scrambling trying to come up with age-appropriate jobs for her. My son has no interest in setting tables or cleaning up the house, so we're waiting until he discovers the usefulness of these activities. If we forced chores onto him, we'd delay such discoveries, and it would take a lot of work and bitterness to overcome his reluctance that we'd have caused in the first place.

USING BLOCKS OF TIME

I've noticed that when my parents are with my kids, they are just *with* them—they're not trying to get them to do stuff like get dressed or eat, and their attention isn't split between my kid and doing other things around the house like cleaning up or prepping meals. I think this is part of the reason why kids like their grandparents so much—it's time with a knowledgeable and skilled person who can help them unlock and explore exciting things about the world without the constant interruptions and distractions that come from someone who is trying to manage them.

Sometimes, I imagine I'm a grandparent and that I don't have anything else to do but be with my kid, following their whims, their agenda, and, most importantly, not trying to get them to do (or not do) anything.

Emulating grandparents and introducing more agenda-free periods is a way to make incremental change across time rather than in terms of changing individual rules. If you can't imagine relaxing any particular rule, perhaps you can just build in some extra time during which the kid's agenda is paramount.

Just experimenting with adjustments that help kids get what they want sends a powerful message. You directly contradict the Greedy Child Fallacy when you work to make life better for them and treat them like they deserve a better life.

BABY STEPS WITH BABIES

Unlike with older kids, when it comes to babies, you don't have to worry about gradually integrating the Taking Children Seriously philosophy into how you raise them. A baby is the ultimate blank slate. You simply encourage any exploration that a baby embarks on. When a baby reaches to grab, tries to roll over, or aspires to crawl, I would support this exploration with brightly colored toys and clear a path so it's easy for them to move. I would set up gates on the stairs, not to block exploration of the stairs, but to make it easy to set the baby on the floor without worrying about a tumble down the steps. If the baby does want to explore the stairs, open the gate but sit close with arms at the ready so you can catch them.

If one of the baby's early food preferences is chocolate, I would recognize the seriousness of that preference as a foundational engagement with the world. I'd hold back the urge to limit this sweet, and instead wait for a problem to appear with eating chocolate. Maybe she'll only eat a bite or two. Maybe she'll eat a lot today but be tired of it tomorrow. Or next week.

If the baby likes screens, is there really anything wrong with swiping at a colorful slab of glass? If she starts to recognize characters and engage with the content, isn't that an encouraging sign of cognitive development? If you're worried that swiping at the screen will grow into a fixation with the screen to the exclusion of books, why not wait and see if that happens? And if they do prefer the screen to books, is that so bad? Are books so important for babies that it's worth stunting their growth in other areas? If an uncle can't outcompete a screen, maybe that's on the uncle? Who needs to adapt their interpersonal skills, a baby or a grown person?

I'M CONVINCED, BUT WHAT ABOUT MY SPOUSE?

Parents rarely agree 100 percent about how to raise their kids, so disagreements about implementing Taking Children Seriously are not unique in this regard.

Persuasion is always possible; no one is ever permanently unable to be convinced. Therefore, trying to figure out if a person is convincible, or worse, convincing yourself that they are not, is wasted effort.

Persuasion might always be possible, but the method of persuasion matters. Simply stating good reasons is rarely enough.

People are not typically persuaded by a direct assault on their positions, even if done courteously. And people are rarely persuaded in a hurry. It's rare that a person is persuaded all at once, where there's a sudden "aha" moment such that they shift from skeptic to convert.

Often the most effective persuasion comes from observing a real-world problem get unambiguously solved. If you can solve problems with your kids to your spouse's satisfaction, you will definitely get his or her attention, at least for the moment. If you can then describe or illustrate the principles underlying your method, you've taken an important step—even if the spouse is still not fully convinced.

Any step is a win, and it's more important to continue to accumulate wins than to achieve some sort of philosophical conversion. I would celebrate the wins in their own right, hold on to them, and take care not to poison future wins—such as rubbing it in.

Shame is the third rail of persuasion. If you make your spouse feel ashamed, then he or she has excellent reason to resent you, leaving you with an entirely avoidable and glaring issue sitting right in the middle of your relationship and the family dynamic.

To bypass this potential pitfall, make it clear that you know you are fallible. You are not insisting you have the answers, and your ideas can be wrong and certainly improvable. You are not presenting the final word on a parenting philosophy. Understand that parenting without rules is radical: It violates almost every norm about raising kids, will likely contradict your spouse's own experience as a child, and will run against the pressure they are getting from their parents and extended family. Any flexibility that you earn from your spouse on these issues is a victory in its own right for which you should feel grateful. I would work on not getting annoyed at your spouse's reflexive urge to impose rules.

At the end of the day, conflicts with your spouse are really the same as conflicts with your kids—they come from not knowing how to do it better, and the goal is to discover a solution that works for you *and* your spouse. Just as you don't want kids doing things without understanding the reasons for doing so, you do not want your spouse blindly going along with your parenting ideas. Rather, you want him or her to *understand* them and implement them willingly. And improve on them!

One way to present Taking Children Seriously to a skeptical spouse is to ask that all rules in the house be considered subject to improvement, and any ideas about how to improve them are welcome from anyone in the household. As long as rules are allowed to change and someone makes an effort to think about improvements, you will find some that work to the satisfaction of your spouse and make things better for your entire family. You can't ask for anything more than that.

I'M CONVINCED, BUT WHAT ABOUT MY EXTENDED FAMILY?

It is a rare grandparent who can refrain from telling their adult son or daughter how to raise their kids. (My parents and in-laws are notable exceptions. All of the references in this section are generalizations and hypotheticals.) The well-meaning urge to dispense advice is overwhelming, and even when this urge is suppressed, it's nearly impossible for grandparents to conceal worried comments or faces when they identify what appears to them as a mistake.

Interestingly, these nuggets of wisdom commonly encapsulate authoritarianism that has been effectively packaged for transmission from generation to generation. "Don't let her get away with that." "He needs to learn that life isn't always easy." "She needs to learn that there are rules."

Defying the cultural expectation of parenting by rule enforcement is hard enough, and reforming your own parents on top of it might be a battle that's only worth engaging lightly, if at all. The trouble is that grandparents don't necessarily let you set the terms. Some grandparents expect their grandchildren to pay fealty with greetings, unwanted hugs and pinched cheeks, and generally to stand at the ready to answer questions and listen to blather. Many expect you, the parent, to act as foot soldier, making sure the kid goes through the proper motions before being set free. It's excruciating, particularly if the grandparent is very old or otherwise sweet and well-meaning.

None of this contradicts the previous point that kids' time with their grandparents can be particularly free and open. Like anyone else, grandparents can be exemplars of both freedom and tyranny.

So, what to do? When facing disapproving family members, my approach would be to always preserve my kids' ability to opt out. If they don't want to participate in the traditional rituals of (mandated) respect for elders, I wouldn't make them give unwanted hugs. I might try to mitigate an elder's offense with suggestions such as, "Let's do hugs after she has a chance to get comfortable in a new place."

In general, the same principles of persuading one's spouse apply to one's extended family, though with far less urgency. In fact, it's good to keep in mind that, unlike with your spouse, you really have no obligation to explain yourself to anyone else. This gives you license to choose the terms on which you try to explain your approach to others. However, if you are relying on grandparents to help with child care, then you really do need to offer some guidance. Fortunately, grandparents tend to be generally permissive because they don't have an agenda with their grandkids. I would talk up this advantage that elders have, describing to them how much the kids seem to thrive when they interact with adults who aren't consumed with getting them to do this or that.

I would say something like, "We let the kids eat whatever they want, and we don't make them do things like clean up after themselves. Don't worry about the mess, I'll clean it up when I get home. Just have fun with them!" When this prompts the inevitable skepticism, I respond with, "We're doing something kinda crazy. So far it seems to be working out, so we plan on going with it until we see warning signs. In fact, if you see some warning signs, let me know."

People are more open to new ideas when you acknowledge that an idea is well outside of the norm. It also helps that you are presenting the idea for their consideration, or their temporary acceptance, rather than as a necessity that they take on board. I like asking for criticism, both because criticism is helpful and because it helps alleviate the concerns of skeptics. If they see something going wrong, I'm going to accept their feedback and make adjustments if necessary, not neglect their input. This has the added benefit that, if they can't show something going wrong, then they might consider that maybe the approach isn't so crazy, after all.

Acknowledging the strangeness of the philosophy casts me in a humble light—it highlights that I know I'm trying an experiment, that I'm not some moralizing crusader standing in judgment of the very parenting of which I myself am a product.

Showing your own parents a different parenting technique is an implicit criticism of how they treated you, but hopefully they are open to trying to improve things. I invoke this perspective whenever the subject comes up. "Mom and Dad, you pride yourselves on parenting more reasonably than your parents, and we are carrying on *that* tradition of improvement and progress." I doubt your parents think they were perfect, so you can appeal to that, too: Progress in how we raise our kids is important to all of us, so let's not dismiss possible improvements without giving them a fair hearing.

A MODEL FOR UNRULING

Moving to zero rules may sound radical, but there is actually a well-accepted model for doing this: leaving home for college. Misgivings aside, parents are generally comfortable with withdrawing rules altogether around age eighteen. The real question for parents transitioning to no rules is not if, but when.

Is a sudden change at eighteen years old really a good idea? It's relatively common for even the most seemingly well-adjusted college freshman to fall apart in some way, drop out, and think themselves to have started real life as a failure, saddled with debt and disappointment. Relative to this dramatic phase change that we all take for granted, is it so radical to wean a child off of rules completely prior to leaving the home?

This is how Taking Children Seriously isn't just different, it completely inverts the conventional view on childhood, which starts children off wrapped with restrictions and limitations and sets them free only years later when they are faced with real responsibilities. Taking Children Seriously sets children free from the beginning, when their parents are around to catch them if they fail. Over time, this authentic engagement with the world on their own terms will build up the necessary knowledge and skills to handle responsibilities such as living on their own, securing a career and future savings, supporting their own dependents, and integrating into a community.

WASHOUT PERIODS

The unschooling movement describes the changes that kids go through when they are liberated from school. They often loaf about for weeks, even months, showing little direction or interest. This can be quite alarming to parents. But it takes time for a kid to trust that they are truly free to do what they want, and that when they engage with adults, they don't have to guard against being forced to accept the adults' agenda. And it takes time for one's creative energies to awaken to the fact that they don't need to dance around expectations, that their own interests are no longer frivolous distractions, and that the adults in their lives will not only not stand in their way, but that they will make an effort to support those interests. After a while, unschooled children tend to find a passion, often one that is outside the bounds of what is considered typical or normal. This leaves them with a competitive advantage when pursuing a career because, while their counterparts are all bullying themselves to ignore distractions and compete for the normal jobs and careers, the unschooled kids are doing something scarce, for which motivation comes easy, and which has real value to the people who share this passion. Even the most eccentric passions have lots of enthusiasts, and in an increasingly globally connected world, it is getting easier and easier to deliver value to a niche market. Many unschooled kids take community college courses and enroll in college in order to get the expertise and credentialing necessary to develop their passions. What seems like loafing around is really a period of washing out ideas that otherwise suppress kids' natural creative energy.

CONCLUSION

The most durable barrier to removing rules is fear.

I got a strong taste of this fear long before I ever had kids. Fresh out of college, I was an idealistic middle school teacher with a vision for setting kids free in the classroom. I aimed to create an oasis of freedom, and I thought they'd be so appreciative that they'd do anything I asked. I was so naive that I was genuinely shocked when they walked all over me. Each day was a slow-motion nightmare, and I struggled for the rest of the year to gain some semblance of control. I learned the reasoning behind the expression "Don't smile until Christmas." A teacher can shift from being a hard-ass into a softy, but not in the other direction.

The key classroom discipline is *consistency*. You absolutely cannot crack, not for a second, because as soon as kids catch a glimpse of leniency, they will push hard, and you will expend energy battling them. If instead you show only an impenetrable wall, they will give up hope of finding a crack and resolve themselves to accepting your dominance.

I was *afraid* of another year facing off against these devious little monsters who, I now believed, were programmed by human nature to find and exploit my weaknesses. (In truth, they were innocently seeking an escape from control, not deviously trying to make me miserable.) How was I, a teacher who had gotten into the game because I had wanted to open up the world to kids, going to reinvent myself as a hard-ass?

Looking back, I can see that the real problem was not naivete but the simple contradiction of trying to foster freedom in a compulsory environment. Freedom is not incompatible with human nature, but it *is* incompatible with locking kids in a building all day and forcing them to learn math. The rationales that I had accepted were not truths about the real world but instead were rather obvious fictions that many of us pretend to believe, in the way that fans of professional wrestling pretend to believe the show isn't fake. Pretending to believe school works enables parents to go to work thinking their kids are in good hands, and teachers to conceal their tyranny over little people with masks of respectability and high moral standing. (Some of them no doubt are respectable and moral, but not simply because they command the attention of a captive audience.)

Imposing rules and enforcing them through physical and psychological dominance is a decisive advantage, the ultimate ace in the hole. Giving it up is scary. It leaves you vulnerable and without a backup plan. It puts you at risk of the ultimate failure: being a bad parent. Of course, you can always fail with and *because* of rules, but rule enforcement grants you the excuse that at least you tried in the socially acceptable way. You did not neglect your kids. You may have failed, but you didn't fail *them*.

When our first daughter began to toddle, I felt the rationales from my teaching days well up within me. As I learned about Taking Children Seriously, I feared that if I let the mask slip, my daughter would be battling me, not just for the year, but for the rest of my life. If I started off as a softy, I'd never regain an edge.

Taking Children Seriously requires parents to overcome this fear. The way to overcome fear is through knowledge—good reasons are reassuring. The essential challenge of this book is to provide a reason that is so appealing that you feel comfortable giving up the decisive advantage of imposing your will. Rule enforcement is like a reassuring tool, and hopefully I've shown that this tool is actually a liability, that both you and your kids are better off without it. It's actually a bigger risk to use the tool than to drop it. What should we replace it with? The same tool we use with adults.

Most people have realized that, in the realm of their adult relationships, attempting to control others is not only futile, it is relationship-destroying. It is also morally wrong. We control children because we *can*, not because it is right. Our decisive advantage is also a destructive one. Even if we could wield psychological superiority against other adults in our lives, we wouldn't, because relationships wrought by manipulation lack richness and depth, the very reasons for building relationships in the first place.

Chapter Ten

PHILOSOPHICAL UNDERPINNINGS

THE RECOMMENDATIONS IN THIS BOOK DON'T COME from "the research." They don't come from my experience or from a sense of what's right. Rather, they come from a theory of knowledge, or what is known in philosophy as *epistemology*. It may seem strange that a theory of what knowledge is and how it grows can serve as an organizing framework for parenting, but that's only because knowledge is so poorly understood.

My goal in this chapter is to show that parenting can be more formally described as stewarding the growth of knowledge in children. To explain the connection, I first need to describe our best theory of knowledge: *critical rationalism*, as developed by twentieth-century philosopher Karl Popper.

Karl Popper is to knowledge what Charles Darwin is to biology, except that Popper's contributions have been largely forgotten. The comparison is more than just a rhetorical analogy—Popper drew connections between his mechanism of knowledge growth and Darwin's mechanism of evolution, natural selection.

Critical rationalism says that knowledge functions in the same way that genes function in biology. Genes are solutions to the problems of survival and reproduction. For giraffes, genes created longer necks that solved the problem of food scarcity by reaching leaves that are high above the ground. Genes created eggs with shells to solve the problem of embryos drying out when birthed on land. Indeed, every biological structure and behavior solves a problem pertaining to survival and reproduction.

It is the same for human knowledge—everything we know is a solution to a problem.

The *mechanism* of the growth of human knowledge parallels that of genetic knowledge. In broad strokes, genes solve new problems via variation and natural selection. Genes constantly mutate as they replicate across successive generations. While most of these mutations are harmful, sometimes a mutation solves a problem of survival in the gene's environment better than other versions of that gene. When that happens, the mutated version of the gene is preserved and spread among the subsequent generations at the expense of the other versions of that gene. In principle, this process is without end—life can continue to solve new problem after new problem by way of mutations and natural selection forever, producing endless varieties of biological forms and behaviors.

Human knowledge growth is likewise the story of solving an endless sequence of problems through a process of variation and selection. But with human knowledge, the problems are not limited to survival—they can be about anything, either in the real world or imagined. And instead of mutation, the engine of variation is *conjecture*, or creative guesswork. Selection consists of, first, *criticizing* all of our candidate guesses and, second, choosing only the guess that seems to work best. Often, this involves actually trying out the guess in the real world to see if it solves the problem in question.

The process of human knowledge growth may be most evident in science, where the conjectures are better known as hypotheses, the criticisms as experiments. It's no surprise that Popper began as a philosopher of science and only later realized that his description of scientific knowledge growth generalizes to all domains, such as art, politics, and morality. Artists make guesses at which brushstrokes and colors go where, and they keep those changes that make the painting more beautiful and discard those that don't. Politicians suggest new policies to address societal problems, and voters criticize those policies on election day. And on the individual level, we're all constantly choosing among conflicting actions and checking to see how those choices match our moral values.

It is this generalization from the philosophy of science to knowledge writ large that makes Popper's theory so consequential. Sadly, it is precisely this generalization that is largely unknown.

Popper's process has a common sense understanding: critical rationalism can be thought of as the idea that guessing and testing, trial and error, applies to all human endeavors. Interestingly, this characterization carries the stigma of being simplistic, childish, or brutish, even though it captures the essence of epistemology better than entire volumes of philosophy. This ignoble characterization of guessing and testing might be the reason Popper's work never took hold outside of science.

Guesswork is lighthearted and fun, but as a reliable source of knowledge, it makes people uneasy. It seems too precarious a foundation upon which to build our understanding of the world. But random genetic mutation may seem like a precarious way to design well-adapted life-forms that can solve high-stakes problems of survival across an infinite number of circumstances. And yet that is precisely what has happened for billions of years.

With each new offspring, genes have a new opportunity to try out different mutations that span the entire space of biological designs. Considering the staggering number of offspring that have ever existed, improbable successes have had ample opportunity to emerge and demonstrate their fitness. Similarly, when guesses at solutions in human affairs flow freely across the infinite range of possibilities (when people are able to try out as many "mutated" ideas as they wish), solutions can pop up that are so well-suited to the problem that we may wonder why we didn't realize it before. Notice the deep connection between freedom and the growth of human knowledge—the former is a *prerequisite* of the latter.

But freedom alone is not enough. Just as genetic variants are culled by their environment, so our candidate solutions must be winnowed down by intense criticism. Effective winnowing must focus solely on whether the candidate solutions truly solve the problem in question. For a process like guesswork to be reliable, bad guesses must be rooted out quickly. And most guesses are indeed bad. Criticism, like conjecture, must be given freedom to operate. It must not be hamstrung by taboos or the hurt feelings of those who rely on the eminence of their stature.

In short, for human knowledge to grow, we can't limit conjecture or criticism. We can't gatekeep new ideas according to where they come from or on whose authority they rest. Instead, they must be judged only on whether they solve the problem at hand.

KNOWLEDGE NEEDS NO AUTHORITY

This all may seem highfalutin and removed from everyday life, but nothing could be further from the truth. Our daily lives present us with a series of problems, conflicting options, and decisions. Do we wake up or sleep in? Have coffee or tea? Eat a filling breakfast or take a snack for the road? Our minds produce a constant stream of candidate solutions—conjectures—as well as a stream of criticisms. "Maybe I'll sleep in and take the morning off? No, I did that last week and my boss got angry. Maybe I'll just sleep for five more minutes?" When solutions work well, we keep using them until a better idea comes along, or until circumstances change.

We are all growing knowledge throughout the day. Often, this might not look like much, especially when we rely on habits and background knowledge that we take for granted. But even when we are going about our day as usual, we constantly encounter new circumstances and ideas, and we always have the choice to modify our routine. Ideally, we welcome these changes as opportunities to make things better, to improve our habits, to discover novel interests and possibilities.

This theory of knowledge stands in stark contrast with the conventional view that our knowledge is what has been justified by the evidence, the research, or some authority on whom we can rely because they hold a particular virtue, often signaled by a degree or credential. This mistaken theory of knowledge, *justificationism,* holds that true ideas can be distinguished from false ones according to which ideas are justified in light of some criteria. Justification typically involves "adding up" the weight of the evidence from "the research" or appealing to the consensus of experts. Once an idea is determined to be justified in this way, it is separated from the unjustified ideas and added to the stack of ideas called knowledge. Experts gatekeep this stack and try to keep it clean of falsehood, thereby presuming that our knowledge is pristine, without error, Truth with a capital T.

This conventional view of knowledge has many flaws. For one, justification always needs an authority: "Justified according to whom or what?" Fortunately, most thinkers today recognize the fallacy of appealing to authorities, as it leads to an infinite regress. For each authority, we can simply ask again, "Authority according to whom or what?" In the past, this line of questioning would stop at the priestly class, who could claim investiture with the Ultimate Authority.

Modern justificationists hold no truck with divine authority, but they've replaced the priests with "the" data, or "the" evidence, or "the" observations. But this just raises the same pesky question—who decides what counts as evidence? Our observations don't come prepackaged with instructions for how to interpret them. If they did, we could just read those instructions (though we'd have to wonder why *those* instructions and not any alternative). Early people interpreted the observation that night follows day as evidence that the sun revolves around the earth. Later people reinterpreted the same observation as evidence for the opposite. Who is right? Who is the high priest of evidence? Today, the fashion is to use complicated math and statistics to calculate who is "probably" right, and so researchers and statisticians have become our new priests who interpret the Book of Nature for us, mulling over their esoteric formulas and then letting us all know what they've decided.

Critical rationalism says that explanations are never justified. Rather, candidate explanations are "simply" conjectured, and then we come up with reasons why any of them might be wrong. In criticizing all of the candidate theories on offer this way, we tentatively discover which of the explanations best account for the evidence. Evidence is still crucial, but it always comes *after* the conjecture.

The theory that the earth revolves around the sun is correct not because of the weight of evidence, but because that theory best accounts for many other observations, such as the motions of other planets and stars.

No authority, no justification is required during this entire discovery process. Instead, we simply and tentatively go with the explanation that best accounts for everything we observe.

The second flaw in justificationism is that, if knowledge must be justified, then conjecture gets a bad reputation. "Mere guesswork" is the opposite of justification, and so justificationists think that "mere guesses" should be dismissed and systematically cleared from the "serious work" of figuring things out. They mistakenly think that guesses are only worth considering *after* they've been justified. But this serves to limit the supply of new ideas and new solutions, weighing them down by a kind of irrational taboo. Justificationism blunts progress by making new ideas harder to come by, and existing ideas get shielded from criticism and improvement—after all, they've already been justified!

Justificationism's third flaw is its view of mistakes and improvement. Mistakes are always embarrassing in the justificationist model, because mistakes mean that the source of knowledge is not reliable. What's worse, when knowledge has been deemed truly justified, that means it cannot be mistaken and therefore cannot be improved. Justified knowledge marks the end of progress. However, in Popper's model, knowledge is never justified, it is never validated as true, and therefore mistakes are treated as *inevitable*. In fact, as we grow knowledge and make progress, mistakes proliferate. As we solve problems, we discover new, better errors that we were not previously in position to resolve. So, the faster we solve problems and grow knowledge, the more errors we'll make. Mistakes are the smoke that signals the fire of progress. Learning is a process of correcting mistaken guesses at solutions until we find a guess that works. And mistakes can even be useful, as they might trigger new ideas that otherwise would not have occurred.

Taking Children Seriously is simply the recognition that, in the realm of parenting, the source of knowledge does not determine its validity, that knowledge does not require authoritarian justification. On the contrary, knowledge creation is an entirely egalitarian enterprise—anyone's conjecture might solve the problem at hand, anyone's criticism might be reason to choose one path over another. Kids' ideas are just as valid as adults', and they should be taken seriously and accounted for in any solution to any conflict.

POPPER AND PARENTING

One of Karl Popper's famous maxims is that all life is problem-solving. Parenting is teaching children how to live, which means how to solve problems. Fortunately, children have the same problem-solving engine that adults have—a mind that produces guesses and can work through criticisms internally. In fact, this creative guessing machine tends to be more active in children because they have not yet learned to be ashamed of their guesses, to mistrust them, or to self-censor them.

To be sure, children are ignorant of the background knowledge that adults have, but that's what childhood *is*—the process of building up sufficient background knowledge so that they don't need an adult to take care of them.

Consider this thought experiment to drive the point home. Imagine a nine-year-old who has figured out how to make money by doing odd jobs for the neighbors, like mowing lawns and doing housework. Imagine he earns enough to pay for his own needs, that he likes to buy and prepare his own food, clothes, and personal effects. We can imagine that he came up with this idea from watching a YouTuber who earns a living doing the same. Imagine another YouTuber gets him interested in coding, and he develops some basic skills by using various games and apps that teach coding. Imagine he apprentices with a local company to apply what he's learned and has the rudiments of a career track in front of him. Imagine that he is also interested in emotional mastery, and he follows a YouTuber who teaches techniques for avoiding getting overly emotional. Imagine he regularly seeks your advice on all of these matters and takes it to heart. He readily tells you about things that are strange or worrisome to him, and when you identify something dangerous, he takes this seriously and investigates strategies to avoid it.

If he has money, if he can get around on a bike or ride public transportation or even hail rides with Uber, if he has an idea for a reliable career, if he can feed and clothe himself, and if he has discernment about dangerous things and trusted people to talk to, he can function as an adult. What I'm describing sounds like a kind of general-purpose prodigy only because our culture doesn't allow children to make so much progress on their own. But there is nothing in principle preventing a nine-year-old from becoming a functional adult. If the boy attains the requisite knowledge to solve new problems as they arise—which he can, just as any other person can—then there is nothing stopping him.

If raising a child is a matter of supporting the child's knowledge acquisition, then getting the right theory of knowledge is crucial. Parenting is applied epistemology.

We now have a philosophical basis for the kind of parenting described in this book. Specifically, we should avoid the pitfalls of bad epistemology (justificationism) and appeal to the strengths of good epistemology (Popper's critical rationalism).

THE BUCKET THEORY OF KNOWLEDGE

The conventional view is that knowledge is taught or acquired from the outside, that it is poured into the mind like water pouring into a bucket. Popper called this the *bucket theory of knowledge*. He exposed how it is reflected in our language: We speak of kids "absorbing" lessons in school, "picking up ideas," and "getting it into their heads."

The general pedagogy, therefore, is to expose children to the "right" ideas—those that have been justified—and to shield them from wrong, unjustified ideas, and hoping that the right ideas "stick." In a controlled setting like school, this means conjecture and guesswork are forbidden. After the exposure, kids are asked to spit out replicas of the same ideas that were "poured in" to demonstrate that they've acquired them. Success is judged by whether the output sufficiently matches the exposure. Output that doesn't match is mistaken, erroneous, failure.

But knowledge never comes from the outside, just like the genetic changes of biological evolution are never acquired from the environment. When genes "learn" to adapt to their environment, they must *first* mutate, and only *then* does the external environment select which among the genetic variants is best adapted to it. In the same way, the creation of all human knowledge requires *first* conjectures, and only *then* do we check these conjectures against internal criticisms and the external world.

All understanding is built up inside of the individual's mind. This process is critically dependent on feedback from the outside, but the building—the conjecturing—itself happens internally. Learning is a sovereign act.

For example, if I stop and ask a local for directions, it might seem like the local is pouring knowledge into my mind when he tells me to go straight until I come to the stoplight and then turn right. But what he's really doing is vibrating the air with his vocal cords, which in turn vibrates my eardrums, triggering electrical signals that travel along my auditory nerves into my brain. I then need to separate those signals out from the background noise, and then conjecture the meaning of the words and syntax *as the local meant them*. Next, I need to creatively guess an internal representation, a mental model of streets and stoplights. The local simply can't insert the model he has in his mind directly into mine.

If the local has a thick accent, then the words will sound very different. I will need to guess that the sounds "turn height" mean "turn right." If he makes grammatical errors, I need to guess what the appropriate grammar would be. If his hand gestures left when he says right, I need to guess which perspective he's referring to. All this guessing isn't some frivolous sideshow, it is the central process to what I'm doing. Whenever I ask directions, I go on high alert to focus my attention so that I can make lots of guesses in rapid fashion, and simultaneously guess critiques of those guesses, so I can weed out the mistakes and produce an accurate mental model.

Even in this simple example, the enormous amount of guesswork is unavoidable. It's not surprising, then, that this process so often fails. In fact, it's amazing that it works at all.

Viewed in this Popperian light, children's learning is all the more incredible because, while they are building the background knowledge that you and I take for granted, they are also figuring out how to use language, how to use emotions, how to use their body, and how to interact with other people. By adult standards, children are astonishing learners. We would be in awe of an adult friend who learned in four years what a four-year-old has learned in their short lifetime.

The bucket theory of knowledge isn't just partially wrong, it is completely wrong. *All* new knowledge comes from within and none from without. Knowledge is always created, never consumed. Therefore, creativity is central to all understanding. It's not a sideshow or a pastime. It's not just for people who indulge in the arts or eccentrics who tinker in their garage. It is at the core of what makes humans unique, something we all use all the time as life throws problem after problem at us. Creativity has produced every new idea that led us from the caves to the moon.

The main reason that some people are more creative than others is not that they were born that way. It's that they have not learned, via shame, punishment, or simple conformity, to suppress it.

REJECTING IDENTITY ESSENTIALISM AND HUMAN NATURE

The notion that a major project in life is to find one's true self is a harmful idea. People don't have a true self, essential and unchanging, and life is not a journey in search of it.

Popper's epistemology shows why: a true, essential, and unchanging self would represent an ultimate truth, one that can't be altered or improved upon.

Let's imagine you've found your true self. How would you know? How would you know that this true self won't change? How would you know when your journey of discovery is complete? The typical answers to these questions—you know when you know; you can feel it in your guts, heart, or bones—reveal their irrationality. "You know when you know" is obviously circular. And why, exactly, are these internal organs so prescient? We are told about mystical experiences that signal self-discovery, which, handily, are not describable in words.

These prescriptions tell people to be their own authorities on who they are—which sounds superficially wonderful, except that we do not *have* some essential, true nature. Instead, we are problem solvers, each capable of becoming enthralled with some particular problem(s). Making progress on a problem situation that we care deeply about is how one lives a satisfying life. Falling in love with a problem requires learning and discovery, and it will proceed in unknowable ways. A person enthralled with music might delve into building musical instruments and then shift from there into sound design for film or find an overlap with physics. Or, a person's passions might drastically change when they encounter something new and unexpected.

Fortunately, living life as a fun, dynamic process of engaging with better and better problems can begin today. There is no need to hold real life in abeyance until one's true self is revealed. The real work begins now.

And this work can quickly take you to the edges of human knowledge. If your dream is to visit other planets, then you'll need to learn a lot about mundane topics like gravity, entrepreneurship, and engineering—about which humanity has discovered rather deep theories.

In contrast, life as a journey of self-discovery is a model of stasis. The journey maximizes experiences, travels the world, and tries out various life partners and living situations. Adherents to this model often spend a lot of time in school, waiting for the self to reach some end state that only then can apply itself to a suitable problem in the external world. There is a lot of psychological and physical activity going on, but this apparent dynamism is illusory. There is lots of discovery in the sense of sampling, but relatively little knowledge growth. Although both the world traveler and advanced degree holder may know a lot, they likely do not know much that isn't already known. On the other hand, the person tinkering in their basement, consumed with a problem while uninterested in self-discovery, is more likely to produce something utterly novel and meaningful.

An injunction to self-discovery can feel profound and mystical, and its appeal to young people is featured in film, music, and fashion. It is held up as a marker of individualism and stands in contrast against communitarian group identification. Individualism is indeed worth celebrating, but not like this. It is better to support individualism with respect and support for an individual's tastes and preferences. Replace "find yourself" with "develop your tastes and preferences."

What about human nature? Isn't there a part of us that is durable, unchanging through the generations, and captured by some of the great wisdom traditions? Isn't it a good idea for kids to inquire about and get familiar with these fundamental and indelible traits?

The idea of an indelible human nature runs counter to Popper's refutation of an essential, permanent self. All of our characteristics, even those obviously tied to survival instincts such as fear of heights or distaste for moldy foods, can be consciously repurposed to inspire skydivers and cheese lovers. Defenders of human nature as a concept tell us that skydivers and cheese lovers are rare examples of culture overpowering nature, but if culture can overpower human nature, then human nature is not the indelible, timeless constant it is made out to be. Instead, it can be changed, and even directly rebutted, if a person develops a reason to do so. Some people become celibate, some become ascetics, some become obsessed with various fads and social conventions, all of which challenge the idea that we are tied to some timeless set of values, instincts, or behaviors.

I raise this because the concept of human nature plays a sinister role in childhood. Chapter Four describes the damage that rules impose on children's relationship with themselves, and the concept of a base inner nature is used to justify the need for an adult to manage a child's affairs. In this view, the adult is necessary to protect children from the depravations of their own innate, animalistic urges. As the child grows, they need to develop their own internal control mechanism that can contain and constrain their nature. Until that mechanism develops, the parent is morally required to keep the child's human nature in check.

Today, the need to control human nature is reified in psychology and neuroscience by way of the function of the brain's frontal lobe. The argument is that the frontal lobes of the brain constrain impulses and are essential for applying the restraint and inhibitions necessary to make good judgments. The frontal lobes aren't fully developed until one's early twenties, and so many psychologists provide a supposedly scientific reason not to take people seriously until then.

But if this science settles the matter, then why is it so common for some adults to be in the thrall of their impulses well past the point at which their frontal lobes have developed? And why is it so common for some teenagers to demonstrate enormous restraint in certain areas, and sometimes in most areas of life? A teenage ball player can be discriminating in when and how they pass the ball and not simply kick at it single-mindedly. A teenage musician can be discriminating in when and how to play the right notes and not just bang at the keyboard. And teenagers often excel at navigating social situations with grace and courteousness. In each of these situations, the teenager has learned restraint as a by-product of learning about the subject at hand. They have *reasons* for making judicious choices, and they make them joyfully, without internal conflict. There is no battle with human nature; there is simply the acumen that comes with understanding. Restraint is not about containing urges; it is about having reasons to do something else.

We don't have a flawed human nature, an inner brute, in need of control. We instead have many competing ideas about what to do next, including desires for quick gratification as well as for long-term goals. The way to select the best choice is to compare the reasons for those choices, not to blindly and forcibly reject those we label as brutish and declare war on them.

WHY CHILDREN ARE AS SPECIAL AS ADULTS

Are children the same as adults? Yes and no.

Clearly, in some ways children are the same as adults (they're both bipedal primates with opposable thumbs), and in some ways they're not (size, strength, and fund of knowledge). The better question is, which of those differences matter? Men and women differ in terms of size and strength, but those don't matter when considering their status as a full person, deserving of the entire suite of human rights, dignities, and privileges.

A typical objection to full personhood for children is that they lack the knowledge to make their own decisions. First, this argument has notoriously failed when applied to other historically marginalized groups. Second, we don't use knowledge tests to apportion human rights. Instead, a person is either fully sovereign, or else is limited in some clearly defined way, such as a prisoner or a dementia patient whose affairs are managed by a legal guardian. With rare exceptions, it would be immoral to force a developmentally delayed adult to eat and sleep in a certain way.

What defines a person? Conventional arguments point to something unique among humans, like divine creation or a soul, or to behavioral features like language or tool use. Some theories appeal to anatomy, noting we are the only bipedal primates with opposable thumbs. None of these arguments have been wholly satisfying, and the debate about what makes a person continues.

Working from Popper's epistemology, David Deutsch identified the difference that counts. People are the only living beings that create unlimited knowledge.

Nonhuman animals can give the appearance of knowledge creation, but this is an illusion. Animals' DNA has programmed them to have the capacity to learn only a narrow set of things from their environment. Said another way, the animals' minds are not the source of these new pieces of knowledge—their brains are utter slaves to their DNA program. Without people, smart animals like chimpanzees and octopi will never make it to the moon. After all, none of their DNA codes for anything close to the biological machinery or behavior that would get them there.

Our machines can be programmed and trained as well, but they cannot create knowledge themselves. We can build machines that learn from the environment, like a Roomba learning a floor plan, or a chess bot learning from old chess games, but the Roomba cannot decide on its own to learn chess—like a nonhuman animal, it is forever enslaved to its program. Recent advances in artificial intelligence give the appearance of knowledge creation, but they are instead mixing and recombining existing knowledge and presenting it to human users.

However, although knowledge creation is unique to humans, uniqueness alone doesn't carry a special moral status. Knowledge creation is special because it is the basis of having an understanding of values, of having preferences, and of being able to suffer and prosper. Like all emotions, suffering and joy depend on the relevant understanding. For instance, my mother generally suffers while reading philosophy but enjoys gardening. Her suffering could turn to joy if reading philosophy became relevant to her intrinsic interest in gardening. If she discovered that the greatest gardener of our era explained his methods and principles in a philosophical treatise, she'd read it with keen eyes.

This line of argument may be hard to swallow. Fortunately, David Deutsch has developed a more objective way to see the connection between knowledge creation, values, and morality.

Since people can create unbounded knowledge, we can utterly transform any environment. We are already transforming the earth, and there's nothing stopping us in principle from transforming the moon, Mars, and eventually the solar system as a whole. In fact, given enough time, knowledge creation may become the dominant phenomenon in the universe, more influential than features like gravity or mass.

Our ability to cause any physically possible transformation means that we can impact anything and everything we care about for the better, from home life to the subcultures to which we belong to how we organize society. It's not wishful thinking to say that our choices and values must account for the existence of people more so than any other living thing. For instance, if we develop moon colonies, we can easily keep dolphins out of it. But there is no way to keep the actions of earthbound *people* out of it. A single person down on earth could develop any number of things that affect the moon colony, such as a new political theory, or a new technology, or a new form of entertainment.

If you care about something, you must also care about people, because people will think up things that could come to affect it. Knowledge creators have consequences for the entire universe, and that gives us cosmic significance. Since children are fully capable of creating knowledge, they are full-status people who are just as cosmically significant as adults.

CONCLUSION: FREEDOM ISN'T OPTIONAL FOR PROGRESS

The mistaken theory that knowledge is justified, and that children are receptacles for knowledge to be poured into, leads to mistaken ideas of control. The conventional view is that we can and should control what children think by carefully removing wrong, unjustified ideas from their consumption. According to this view, if we allow in only what is proven to be true, then children will be set on the right path. This sets the stage for restricting screens, near-constant surveillance, compulsory schooling, and general limitations on autonomy. In short, control the child by controlling what goes into the bucket that is their mind.

This control can't work, because minds are not buckets, and kids will reach unpredictable conclusions even if their inputs are controlled. Attempts to control often backfire in precisely the opposite direction. Some kids take particular interest in the ideas that are restricted simply because they are restricted. When efforts at control do work, it is because some kids will come to understand the reasons for those controls, even if the methods to impart those reasons are misguided. Unfortunately, some kids will only go through the motions, showing the expected behavior but for reasons of fear or shame rather than that they internalized the "right" knowledge.

Just as you've experienced thoughts popping up in your mind, unbidden and seemingly from nowhere, kids also undergo the same process. Like us, they can't know ahead of time what their most compelling thoughts will be. They can only deal with thoughts after they appear, in light of all of the alternative thoughts they might explore. If kids can't even know ahead of time what kind of thoughts will pop into their minds and which they'll choose to explore, how could parents possibly know such a thing? The truth is that they can't, and so there's no way of *controlling* what guesses children's minds might make and passionately pursue.

The central message of this book is that *controlling knowledge growth in people is not possible*, including children. In fact, we should pursue the opposite: freedom. Freedom doesn't mean neglect—it still involves safety, health, and order. But these are achieved while *preserving* kids' autonomy, not at the *expense* of autonomy.

This isn't easy, and there are no simple rules for achieving this, because this requires unpredictable creativity, knowledge growth, and discovery by the parent, but it is a more productive target for a parent's efforts than working to control. Maximizing control and maximizing freedom both take work, but the latter is more fun and less work in the long run because the sovereign child can take care of themself sooner.

Childhood is a period of supported knowledge growth until a person is capable of solving life's problems on their own. Knowledge grows by guessing and testing, trial-and-error elimination, conjecture and criticism. The necessary condition is freedom, where guesses and criticisms are encouraged and given a chance to work, and mistakes are never punished or shamed.

Chapter Eleven

PAST AND FUTURE

IF PEOPLE ARE KNOWLEDGE CREATORS AT BIRTH, WHY did it take humanity tens of thousands of years before progress really began to take off?

Knowledge growth was largely stagnant for the bulk of human history. Humans scraped by with the same hand axes and animal pelts for tens of thousands of years. Even after we established cities and written language, knowledge growth was too slow for people to notice advances during their lifetime.

The conventional answer is that rapid growth required that we break free of religious dogmas and develop the scientific method, and that these developments spawned the Industrial Revolution.

But this still does not answer the question of why it took so long. For example, the ancient Egyptians made tremendous discoveries in mathematics and engineering. Surely a people who could build the Great Pyramids could figure out the scientific method. The same could be said of every ancient civilization. Their artifacts testify to sophisticated understanding of the patterns of the heavens, the biological world, and even political organization. So why did these anatomically modern, creative, problem-solving humans not bring about the Industrial Revolution earlier?

David Deutsch has a fascinating theory: that our ancient ancestors used their creativity to *suppress* new ideas. Rather than try to figure out new solutions to problems, ancient people tried to figure out how to preserve their existing solutions. This not only meant preventing the loss of these solutions but also preventing them from changing at all, including changes that were *improvements*.

Knowledge was precious for ancient people. Unlike all non-human animals, early humans relied on knowledge such as domesticating fire, hunting, and organizing into groups to survive. Crucially, this knowledge needed to be faithfully passed on to the next generation. Clans that didn't have a set of norms for effectively passing along knowledge didn't survive.

Some nonhuman animals pass knowledge between generations, but their method of doing so is different from ours. Young beavers are genetically programmed to seek out the sound of rushing water and to drag elongated objects toward that sound. Adult beavers are said to teach their offspring, but beavers raised in isolation are able to build dams without input from other beavers. Nearly all nonhuman animal behavior, regardless of its complexity, is genetically programmed—the genes carry knowledge from one generation to the next.

A notable exception is tool use among chimpanzees. Young chimps learn by observing others draw insects out of a hole with a stick or knock down a beehive. But the method that chimps use to acquire this knowledge is different from how people do it. As we've seen, people make guesses in their minds that form an understanding, and then they try those guesses out in the world, creatively refining their understanding accordingly.

Chimpanzees, on the other hand, ape each other. They blindly replicate chunks of the process, one movement at a time until they get the succession of movements to work. The idiom of "going through the motions" captures this process, as there is no understanding in the chimp's mind. Transferring knowledge in this way of "dumb" copying requires multiple repetitions, often over years of training. And once obtained, the knowledge cannot be modified. If a chimp uses a stick to pick up ants from a hole, it can't make the mental leap (a guess *is* a mental leap) to use the stick to do something else, like dig seeds out of a fruit or assist with grooming other chimps.

People, on the other hand, make these mental leaps all the time, mixing up applications for tools in various ways because they have a mental model that they can manipulate. They can imagine doing things differently, they can conceive of a never-before-seen future state and then actualize it.

But for ancient people, the capacity to do things differently wasn't regarded as a means by which they might solve new problems and improve their lives. Rather, it was considered a liability that had to be guarded against. Knowledge was so precious that it couldn't be altered, lest it be lost.

How do you prevent a creative mind from trying out new things? You use violence and threats of violence, dogma, taboo, and excommunication. Surely, ancient peoples didn't knowingly employ these tactics to intentionally achieve stasis. Instead, it was likely a natural consequence of our species' ignorance about how to steward knowledge. Only clans with very strict norms about knowledge preservation survived. Clans that had a lax attitude about things they knew, like how to make fire or which berries were poisonous, likely lost that knowledge and didn't survive to pass along these norms. Over time, the means of preserving the ideas, the threats and the taboos, probably became exceptionally fine-tuned, just in the way that genetic knowledge becomes exceptionally fine-tuned to solve problems of biological survival. The taboos become very effective at eliciting shame among violators and conformity among clansmen. The norms themselves gradually became infused with the same supernatural providence and power that were thought to drive the natural world. Questioning the norms amounted to heresy, an insult to the gods as well as those among the clan who communed with them.

Admittedly, progress did occasionally happen, but only when changes for the better occurred too slowly for any individual to notice. In other words, innovations could only "sneak" into society and cause widespread change if they could "bypass" all of the suppressive methods that the culture employed to enforce total conformity. It follows that such innovations necessarily had certain attributes: They fixed themselves in a population on timescales on the order of a generation or longer, they disproportionately impacted aspects of society that the broader culture tended to ignore, and the magnitude of their impact was small enough to remain unnoticed by the society's censors.

Despite our ancestors' pervasive efforts to stifle innovation, ancient people eventually formed cities, achieved technological successes, and established institutions such as mature religions, nation-states, and sophisticated traditions of language and art. But even then, the dominant mode of knowledge transfer focused on preservation and stasis rather than improvement and dynamism. Early civilizations thought that all knowledge came from the past, a fixed quantity that could only decay over generations if the people weren't too careful. The present time was always considered a Fallen Age.

To be sure, preserving knowledge is important. It can indeed be lost, and there are many examples of ancient societies backsliding. Romans living after the collapse of the empire dwelled among the crumbling engineering marvels that they no longer knew how to create or maintain. Authority figures were right to be worried about losses like this.

WHAT CHANGED? WHAT MADE PROGRESS TAKE OFF?

Progress took off when pockets opened up that tolerated, and even encouraged, new ideas. This must have happened a few times in our history as a species, but they ultimately collapsed under external pressure and internal stasis. A remarkable exception was the European Enlightenment of the 1600s and 1700s, because the pockets that opened up *then* have been expanding ever since. The culture of welcoming new ideas, criticizing old ones, and solving problems planted the seeds of the Scientific and Industrial Revolutions that have transformed our world.

Look at any metric of human progress, from life expectancy to energy production to reduction of violence, and you see an explosion shortly after the Age of Enlightenment. In David Deutsch's conception of human history, that is when the West shifted to a tradition of problem-solving and tolerance of new ideas, and especially of criticism in general. Before the 1700s, the story of almost every human who lived was one of crushing stasis, of all-consuming oppression and suppression of new ideas that continually popped into their minds. We are extraordinarily fortunate to have been born after the West went through this tectonic shift. We are spared the violence, oppression, and shame that were imposed on generation after generation for tens of thousands of years.

But in Deutsch's view, we are not finished. The Enlightenment isn't an event in the past, with its list of heroes like Galileo, Bacon, and Voltaire already cast. It is a process that continues today. Shame and dogma and taboo and obeisance to authority are still very much with us, even though their totalitarianism has been toppled. The moral virtue of openness to new ideas has reinforced the Enlightenment with the power of modern science, technology, capitalism, and liberal democracy.

David Deutsch envisions an end state for this process, where all appeals to authority are laughed off as errors of the past, akin to other once-plausible ideas like the flat earth or perpetual motion machines. He calls this a fully dynamic society, in contrast to the fully static societies of the ancients. In a fully dynamic society, the only thing holding back an idea is whether or not it works. Its source, the weight of evidence, and the blessing of an authority are irrelevant with respect to whether it gets used to solve a problem. Mistakes are recognized as inevitable, and while steps are taken to mitigate their impact, they are nonetheless welcomed as a necessary by-product of progress (and often are themselves grist for discovery).

Why does this matter? Because dynamism means progress. If stasis kept early humans in the Stone Age for millennia, then dynamism can get us to unimaginable wealth and prosperity. Today, we are among the very first generations to grow up in a time dominated by freedom in every sense of the word, and we are enormously fortunate that our predecessors did the hard work of jailbreaking our culture from its self-imposed authoritarianism.

WHAT DOES THIS HAVE TO
DO WITH CHILDREN?

Children are central to the project of keeping a culture static. Children must acquire not only the culture's knowledge but also the means of preserving that knowledge unchanged. Children need to take up the shame of nonconformity so effectively that, when they grow up, they will reliably pass it on to their children. The stigma of criticizing authorities and the esteem of honoring them must be powerful enough among children to become the norm among them as adults, generation after generation.

A static society will allow children autonomy, but only in certain areas and only *after* they have sufficiently demonstrated fealty to the static norms. A child who reliably performs their assigned household chores can be given autonomy within that job once they demonstrate that they can and will do it the "right" way.

If, on the other hand, children get a taste of true freedom from the beginning, if they get enjoyment out of solving their own problems in their own way and orient themselves toward interests that don't conform with the majority, then this will need to be driven (often beaten) out of them. This may explain why many adults are so quick to crack down on things that kids find particularly enjoyable. Having an outsized amount of fun almost universally signals a straying from the static norms. Conformity is almost never wildly fun. This is especially true when the source of enjoyment is new, such as a novel form of food, technology, or media. A simple rule of stasis is to be watchful and stamp out excessive enjoyment among children. Any number of charges can be summoned as rationales—temptation, greed, waste, disorder, frivolity, and other devices of sin or Satan.

In Deutsch's view, the authoritarian treatment of children today is a remnant of our ancient past. While most other institutions in the West have adopted Enlightenment values, including once formidable bastions of dogma and taboo like religion or the makeup of the family, our attitudes toward children have been among the last to change. This may seem strange, since it is so common to hear optimistic bromides about how children give our lives meaning and are our hope for the future. But it is also fitting that this key to stasis would be one of the last surviving holdovers.

To be sure, the treatment of children has been getting better, and the progress we've made should be celebrated. But when we look around our culture, it is hard to find a clearer example of a self-imposed shackle that is holding us back.

Unlocking the creative potential of children is a major lever that, once pulled, would lurch us closer toward the prosperity of a fully dynamic society.

HOW WOULD THIS BE TRANSFORMATIVE?

Children represent a huge pool of untapped productivity, particularly teenagers. Primitive societies marked rites of passage into adulthood around age thirteen, while today children experience an extended adolescence that often persists into their twenties. They are warehoused in schools where they have essentially zero productive output and instead are a net drain on the productivity of teachers and parents. The theory is that teenagers are training in school to be extra productive when they join the workforce, but the reality is that they learn almost nothing in school that is essential for most jobs, they arrive in college often unprepared for advanced education, and they are delivered into the workforce with the expectation that they will receive on-the-job training anyway! As Bryan Caplan describes in *The Case Against Education*, school functions as a sorting and labeling mechanism for employers, not as a productivity booster. It delays the time at which kids can engage with real life.

An extended adolescence delays the time at which people can begin to be productive. This forces parents to care for teenagers who could otherwise be caring for themselves, which in turn causes parents to have fewer children. Fewer people means fewer problem solvers, less productivity, and slower progress. It's true that a larger population means more consumption, but people can produce more than they consume, as evidenced by the fact that Earth has more abundance today with our eight billion people than ever before.

Yes, there were problems with exposing children to the demands of adulthood too early. But the problems that had incentivized child labor laws are solvable. Parents should not pressure their kids to take a job they don't want, but they also shouldn't pressure them to be bored at school. Even a menial job offers more freedom than compulsory school. A kid who is bored bagging groceries can quit and find another job. A kid bored in social studies class cannot. Which is more humane? At least the grocery clerk can talk at will, not to mention earn money, gain job training, and access a career ladder that, if the climbing begins in the teenage years, could reach a significant height by the time most students are graduating college, with savings rather than debt. With money in the bank and having had a taste of real life, this young adult is in a much better position to survey their options, consider advanced training or experimentation, and perhaps launch into another phase.

The conventional treatment of children is utopian, as it conceives of a final stage where one obtains a degree and lands the relevant job, usually many years and dollars in the future. In this model, success requires closing one's eyes to competing interests. This has generated a whole segment of the self-help industry that counsels people in ignoring interesting stuff through willpower, self-discipline, self-control, and time management, all euphemisms for self-bullying. Interests are disparaged as distractions.

The approach described here is closer to incremental change, which, as I discussed in Chapter Nine, is Popper's alternative to utopianism. Trying out an apprenticeship or unskilled job that can be easily swapped for something that better matches one's interests and talents is a lower-risk option that has better chances of resulting in a rewarding lifestyle than the utopian approach. Childhood gives us eighteen years of exploring to find something interesting and remunerative.

There is no reason a voluntary apprentice model can't be restored and updated for the modern world. Education could focus on real-world training around genuine interests in a way that is guided by providing value to others.

College graduates, on the other hand, often enter adulthood hundreds of thousands of dollars in debt. This debt forces them to narrow their options to uninspiring jobs rather than taking risks on starting new ventures that might solve problems in novel ways and raise the prosperity of everyone. Instead, college graduates are incentivized to play it safe, to never experiment, and to accept a middling quality of life. This overall outlook—a life of low expectations, where the main virtues are persistence and conformity rather than dynamism—gets passed onto their children as a tragic holdover from the static societies of yesteryear.

Taken together, our treatment of young people is a colossal missed opportunity. We stomp out their creativity, shelter them from engaging in the real world, confuse them with misguided busywork, saddle them with high debt and low expectations, and then set them loose. When they get depressed, we diagnose them with a mental health disease, recommend a therapist to help them accept the status quo, and take away their phones.

Instead, we could be training up a generation of problem solvers with unprecedented productivity. We could be reshaping adulthood around productivity and value. We could be giving them the confidence to chart their own way. We could support them as they align their interests with their careers such that they become valuable to others on their own terms—strangers, colleagues, and eventual families of their own. The biggest impact of liberating children will be unlocking the creativity and productivity of adults.

WE NEED A MOMENT

Our ancestors can certainly be forgiven. Explanatory knowledge—knowledge that accounts for how the world works—is radically new in the universe, and they were the first to ever wield it. Today, things are different. We have good theories of knowledge, and we've largely broken free of the mind-forged manacles of authoritarianism. We need to recognize the power that we are stewarding so that we can appropriately transfer it to succeeding generations in a way that they can use it well. As we saw in Chapter Ten, explanatory knowledge can shape solar systems and galaxies and even the fate of the universe itself.

More directly, we can see that our prosperity today derives from knowledge growth in the past, and expanding prosperity for our descendants depends on what we discover today. If the mini-Enlightenment that sparked in Ancient Greece had persisted, life today would have the features of two thousands years of postindustrial progress instead of just two hundred. Compared to people living in that alternative timeline, our lives today are more impoverished than the lives of the ancients are to us.

The stakes are high. We owe it to our descendants to expurgate static norms as quickly as we can and pave the way toward an extraordinary future.

EPILOGUE

OUR OLDEST DAUGHTER WAS LEANING AGAINST THE glass door and pointing outside. She had recently learned how to walk, and with this came a burst of curiosity about the world. It was 7:00 a.m. on a spring morning, and everything was cold and wet. She wanted to go outside, but I really didn't. As she slapped at the door and babbled about going out, I noticed her demeanor shift from bubbly curiosity to visible annoyance at my refusal to open it. I didn't bother voicing my objection because I knew she wouldn't understand that Daddy likes to be dry and relaxed in the morning and not braced against the cold and wet. So I didn't say anything.

As she continued to slap at the door and demand to go out, I stared blankly at her, thinking. I couldn't just let her be upset—I needed to do something. But I couldn't reprimand her for making a fuss because what did she know? From her perspective, she was locked in a house-shaped box, and her father was mutely standing by instead of helping her get out. I could have distracted her with a game or by horsing around, but I didn't like those options, either. I *wanted* her to go outside and explore. I wanted her to be curious, to experience her first spring, and a part of me definitely wanted to do it with her.

I decided to bite the bullet and take her outside. I reached down and started putting her boots on, but she resisted. She didn't want to put on boots; she wanted to go outside. Was I going to use my grown-up muscles to restrain her, for her own good? "You want to see the planet? Not before I wrestle you to the floor and shove things on your feet." I could imagine telling her that I was putting the boots on so her feet wouldn't get cold, but she could barely talk. She'd never encountered the concept of cold, wet feet. In fact, that's exactly what she was clamoring for—an opportunity to learn just that. So I opened the door, and out she toddled. I snatched my coat and shoved my feet into shoes and dashed after her.

The deck boards were rectangular puddles crusted with a paper-thin layer of ice. She crashed through them like a miniature Godzilla, oblivious to the cold wetness seeping through her pajama feet and up her calves. She sat down in the ice-cold water and excitedly splatted the deck puddles with her hands, utterly uncaring about the water that seeped into her diaper and chilled her bottom. Then she got up and trundled off to the sidewalk and into the neighbor's yard. She put her hands in puddles, grabbed at dirt, and put some of it in her mouth.

She was having a ball, squealing and laughing and stomping around. And, come to think of it, I was having a good time, too. I had drunk coffee and read the news on thousands of mornings, but I hadn't stood outside and breathed fresh morning spring air in a good while. And I'd never seen a new human discover wetness and coldness and ice and dirt for the first time. She got to use her newfound power of walking to see and feel new things. She also learned about something else, that Dad opens doors to fun—literally. And when she's had enough of the coldness and wetness, Dad picks her up and gets her warm and dry.

We were outside for less than ten minutes. When we came in, I plopped my daughter in a warm bath, threw our clothes in the washing machine, and got changed. Later, while sipping my coffee as she splashed around in the tub, I reflected on what had just happened. She'd been right and I'd been wrong— going outside in the cold and wet *was* better than staying inside. She enjoyed the wetness even without boots, and she learned enough about the discomfort of being cold and wet that she might be interested in putting on boots next time. The whole experience was actually delightful. We both got dirty, but we'd both needed to change out of our morning clothes, anyway. And I ended up enjoying my coffee even more so than usual, since I was sipping it over a backdrop of happy child sounds, reflecting on something more profound than the morning news.

ACKNOWLEDGMENTS

NAVAL RAVIKANT IS THE REASON I WROTE THIS BOOK. He inspired me to think I had something worthwhile to say about a subject as ancient and well-worn as parenting. I am enormously grateful for his support for this book and for the philosophy in general.

David Deutsch's ideas have been transformative for me personally, and the ideas in this book are only a part of the whole. His work inspires a commitment to freedom, optimism, and humanity in general that brings brightness to every day.

Sarah Fitz-Claridge has done more than anyone to develop and promote the ideas of Taking Children Seriously. She manages the indispensable takingchildrenseriously.com and has produced a trove of invaluable interviews and talks.

Everything in this book derives from Deutsch and Fitz-Claridge's philosophy, but I do not pretend to speak for them or the movement they started. Any inconsistencies are my errors.

Logan Chipkin is my collaborator and editor, both for clarity of writing and fidelity to the underlying philosophy. Logan has an encyclopedic knowledge and a special talent for distilling an idea down to its essence. I've learned an enormous amount from Logan as a colleague and a friend.

David Kedmey has been especially supportive. He proofread several drafts, made substantial edits, and helped with every stage from conception to printing, all while being encouraging and enthusiastic. He is a model of this book's guiding philosophy.

Lulie Tanett, Brett Hall, and Michael Sharick have helped me refine and sharpen these ideas and helped me work out the specific examples and arguments.

I thank my kids for being such delightful test subjects. They take the challenges of being unconventional in stride. I thank them in advance for dealing with the fact that their father wrote a book about their upbringing.

I thank my parents. Our discussions about how to raise kids started when I was very small, and this book is the culmination of those many conversations. My parents inspire me to make the world better for my kids in the way that they have done for me. They make me proud.

And lastly, my wife is extraordinary. She is one of the rare people who can maintain a fierce seriousness as well as an open mind. She tried out and embraced the radical parenting ideas in this book, found her personal ethos in them, and made them her own. She is the foundation of this book, as she literally makes it all possible as a mother, a wife, a provider, a model of character and integrity, and an intellectual force. And she is enormously fun. She helped me formulate the arguments in every chapter and contributed to almost every real-life example. Thanks to her, I am living a charmed life.

ABOUT THE AUTHOR

AARON STUPPLE is a practicing physician and former public school teacher. He lives in Western Massachusetts with his wife and five children.

Made in the USA
Las Vegas, NV
13 January 2025